For Socialism

by

GUSTAV LANDAUER

Translated by David J. Parent

Introduction by

Russell Berman and Tim Luke

TELOS PRESS

St. Louis 1978

ISBN: 0-914386-11-5 (paper)
        0-914386-10-7 (cloth)

Library of Congress Card Number: 78-51081

Manufactured in the United States of America.

INTRODUCTION

By Russell Berman and Tim Luke

Today, nearly sixty years after his death at the hands of White troops engaged in the suppression of the poorly organized 1919 Bavarian Soviet Republic, Gustav Landauer's works are slowly being recovered from years of abuse and neglect. Until quite recently,[1] he remained virtually unknown except for his ridiculous appearance in

---

1. To be sure, Landauer studies are not to be found in any great number, especially in English. However, Eugene Lunn's excellent *Prophet of Community: The romantic socialism of Gustav Landauer* (Berkeley, 1973) does a detailed and complete analysis of Landauer's thought in addition to blending the course of his philosophical development into a sophisticated discussion of Landauer's own personal life. A less involved and more narrowly focused treatment of Landauer's work can be found in Charles B. Maurer's *Call to Revolution: The Mystical Anarchism of Gustav Landauer* (Detroit, 1971) which concentrates heavily upon Landauer's indebtedness to Fritz Mauthner's linguistic philosophy. An even briefer consideration of Landauer's writings, and one which looks more closely at the Jewish dimension in Landauer, is available in the recently published *Gustav Landauer: Philosopher of Utopia* (Indianapolis, 1977) by Ruth Link-Salinger (Hyman). Clearly, Lunn's study remains the best of these three book-length investigations. Also available are shorter discussions including, Martin Buber, *Paths in Utopia* (Boston, 1958); Paul Breines, "The Jew as Revolutionary. The Case of Gustav Landauer," *Leo Baech Yearbook*, XII, 1967; Thomas Espers, "The Anarchism of Gustav Landauer" (M.A. thesis, Univ. of Chicago, 1961); Sterling Fishman, "Prophets, Poets and Priests: A Study of the Men and Ideas That Made the Munich Revolution" (Ph.D. dissertation, Univ. of Wisconsin, 1960); and C.M., "Gustav Landauer," *Freedom*, anarchist weekly, Vol. 33, No. 16 (April 15, 1972). Of particular importance to an understanding of Landauer's role in the Munich revolution is the anthology edited by Ulrich Linse, *Gustav Landauer und die Revolutionszeit. Die politischen Reden, Schriften, Erlasse und Briefe Landauers* (Berlin, 1974). In Germany a short discussion of Landauer's political legacy is offered in Harry Pross, "Die Aktualität Gustav Landauers" in *Neues Hochland* 66 (1974), pp. 517-533. See also Heinz Joachim Heydorn's introduction to the German republication of Landauer's *Aufruf zum Sozialismus* (Frankfurt, 1967). Indicative of current interest in Landauer's anarchism is the republication of a variety of literary and theoretical texts, for example his *Rechenschaft* (Bremen, 1977); *Entstaatlichung—für eine herrschaftslose Gesellschaft* (Westbeuern, 1975); *Die Revolution* (Berlin, 1974). See also the anthologies edited by Heinz Joachim Heydorn, *Zwang und Befreiung* (Cologne, 1968) and Ruth Link-Salinger-Hyman, *Erkenntnis und Befreiung* (Frankfurt, 1976).

Karl Mannheim's *Ideology and Utopia* in which Mannheim uses Landauer as his whipping-boy for the alleged blind extremism of anarchist utopianism.[2] Indeed, after being prematurely thrown on to the theoretical scrap heap with the fall of the Bavarian Soviet, Landauer has been remembered characteristically as "one of those free spirits" unhappy in any organization,[3] as a proponent of "impractical romantic Anarchism,"[4] and as something of an "excessively romantic"[5] dreamer apparently destined to run afoul of hard political realities. For the most part, only Martin Buber's perennial efforts to keep Landauer's ideas alive as a genuine socialist alternative have done justice to the rich diversity and practical aims of Landauer's theoretical project.[6]

As his *For Socialism* clearly reveals, Landauer is anything but an "impractical romantic anarchist." Continuing the thoughts he first advanced in his *Skepsis und Mystik*[7] and *Die Revolution*,[8] he effectively criticizes the central social forces of modern European society—the Second International, advanced capitalism, modern science, the Social-Democratic Party, orthodox Marxism, and the economistic vision of state socialism—while, at the same time, outlining an emancipatory, stateless, political order grounded in the traditions of organic community. Landauer defines *socialism*, in the only manner that preserves its metatheoretical freedoms, as *faith*, as moral regeneration, and as creative individual activity within an intimate spiritual "community of communities."[9] As a moral idea that gains realization only through willed human activity, Landauer's concept of socialism generates a sophisticated critique of the classical Marxist orthodoxy. Instead of presenting the working classes with "scientific socialist" blueprints that prescribe organizing to effect

2. Karl Mannheim, *Ideology and Utopia* (New York, 1936), pp. 197-198.
3. George Woodcock, *Anarchism: A History of Libertarian Ideas and Movements* (New York, 1962), p. 432.
4. James Joll, *The Second International, 1889-1914* (New York, 1966), p. 64.
5. Woodcock, *op. cit.*, p. 482.
6. Buber edited a collection of Landauer's articles, *Beginnen: Aufsätze über Sozialismus* (Köln, 1924), and in addition to discussing Landauer in *Paths to Utopia*, he remembered Landauer in his *Pointing the Way* (New York, 1957).
7. *Skepsis und Mystik: Versuch im Anschluss an Mauthners Sprachkritik* (Berlin, 1903).
8. *Die Revolution* (Frankfurt a.M., 1908).
9. See Lunn's discussion, pp. 199-213.

short-run reforms while waiting for historical contradictions to produce the inevitable class revolution, Landauer counsels the workers to act immediately, for "Socialism need not come. . . . But socialism can come and should come, when we wish it." [10]

I. *Landauer's Life*

Born in 1870 to a prosperous Jewish family, Landauer attended the gymnasium in Karlsruhe and then studied at the universities of Berlin, Heidelberg, and Strasbourg only to return in 1891 to the more exciting life at the University of Berlin. [11] His strong interest in Nietzsche, his participation in the circles of the Freie Volksbühne (a theatrical organization founded by Bruno Wille to promote working-class cultural awareness) and his involvement with groups of radical socialist students all contributed to his growth during this period. Of particular importance, however, was the influence of the anarchist Benedikt Friedländer, who introduced him to the works of Eugen Dühring, Peter Kropotkin, and Pierre-Joseph Proudhon. [12]

Yet, it was also during these years of 1892-93 that Landauer was coming to terms with Marxism. Associated with the "Berliner Jungen," a group of anti-authoritarian radical students dissatisfied with the Social Democratic Party's (SPD) bureaucratic procedures, Landauer attempted to blend his anarchist and socialist leanings into a unified liberatarian Marxism. Despite some early articles in *Die Neue Zeit*, the anarchist component soon prevailed as can be seen in his first novel, *Der Todesprediger*, which is the earliest expression of his characteristic fusion of vitalistic Nietzschean individualism with socialist communalism. [13] Within the Jungen group, Landauer increasingly sided with the anarchist members and attended the Second International's Zurich Congress in 1893. [14]

Landauer returned to Berlin from Switzerland in February 1893 and took over the editing of *Der Sozialist,* a weekly newspaper originally set up by the Union of Independent Socialists which had

---

10. Quote cited in Lunn, p. 212.
11. Maurer, *Call to Revolution*, p. 25.
12. Lunn, p. 62.
13. *Ibid.*, pp. 45-46.
14. For a discussion of the Zurich Congress and its reception of the anarchists, see Joll, pp. 71-74.

grown out of the Jungen movement. Landauer soon set an entirely anarchist course but lost control of the journal in an internal editorial struggle in 1895-96.[15] He subsequently attended the 1896 International Socialist Congress in London as an anarchist delegate, but was expelled before delivering his speech against the SPD.[16]

Landauer devoted himself to independent research and writing during the years between 1898 and 1908, which were spent partially in prison due to his activities as an anarchist publisher.[17] After working on another novel, *Lebendig tot* in 1899-1900, Landauer published his first major philosophical work, *Skepsis und Mystik* in 1903, in which he treats the mysticism of Meister Eckhart.[18] Literary studies and translations of authors ranging from Walt Whitman to Kropotkin also followed. Landauer's thought matured considerably during this decade, and he soon gave it political expression in *Die Revolution* (1908), "Volk and Land: Thirty Socialist Theses," (1908) which led to the founding of the Socialist Bund[19] and, most clearly, in *For Socialism* (1908-1911). Here ones finds an outstanding example of the dissatisfaction with the rigid institutional structures characteristic of Germany during the period of rapid industrialization following national unification in 1870-71. Despite the broad range of turn-of-the-century cultural movements — naturalism, symbolism, neo-romanticism, *völkisch* thought — most were marked by an antagonism to forms of experience perceived to be antiquated, illegitimate, and oppressively hierarchical. Certainly not all of these voices advocated the emancipation of experience, matter, or the senses from the restrictive limits imposed by society. Nevertheless, the confrontation of form and content, of form and life is the unifying figure of thought underlying the cultural crisis in turn-of-the-century

---

15. Lunn, pp. 118-120. Ultimately, *Der Sozialist* died in 1899 after losing most of its financial support and audience.

16. Gustav Landauer, *Social Democracy in Germany* (London, 1896). For an interesting treatment of how Landauer was refused the privilege of speaking to the Congress and was physically thrown out of the meeting hall in London, see Joll, pp. 74-76.

17. Landauer's prison terms usually proved quite productive. During his short six month sentence for allegedly "libelously" attacking the Berlin police commissioner, he wrote his short novel, *Lebendig tot,* and carefully edited the book by Fritz Mauthner, *Beiträge zu einer Kritik der Sprache* (Stuttgart, 1901), which was to profoundly reorient Landauer's own thinking.

18. Landauer also translated the sermons of Meister Eckhart while in prison.

19. See *Die Zukunft,* 58. Band 56-57.

Germany. For the symbolist poet Stefan George, the communicative and social concerns of Hugo von Hofmannsthal were tantamount to the worst apostasy: the betrayal of the exigencies of form. In a parallel, albeit very different situation, the young Georg Lukács quite consistently defended a neo-classicist position; culture, as meaningful life, became possible only by way of the formative force provided by a renunciation of chaotic, immediate experience. Yet, even where the chaos of life seemed most threating, its seductive power remained a force which an overly repressive culture increasingly had to confront. Gustav von Aschenbach, the classicist, the admirer of Frederick the Great, is drawn to Venice and his death; but this is not simply an individual's demise. It is also the crisis of nineteenth century European culture in general. For, as Thomas Mann realizes, European order cannot resist the temptations of the Venetian siren at the gateway to Asia.

This diffuse opposition to the forms of established society corresponded to a widespread dissatisfaction with the specific character of modernization in Germany. Not only industrialization, but also the strengthening of bureaucracy and the increased centralization of the political system disrupted traditional social ties and led to urban isolation, which all fed the flames of criticism. Landauer's significance lies in his recognition of the issues and, perhaps, more importantly, his understanding that most of the German left would be utterly incapable of speaking to them. Consequently, in a political landscape increasingly monopolized on the left by the Social Democrats, Landauer reorganized the journal *Der Sozialist* in 1909 in order to further the cause of the Socialist Bund and, with the growing threat of war, to promote pacifism and combat chauvinism. In 1917, he left Berlin to move to the small Swabian town of Krumbach where he remained until November 1918 when Kurt Eisner summoned him to revolutionary Munich. After Eisner's assassination in February 1919, he was appointed Minister of Culture and Education in April. Within a week, however, a military soviet government was established under the leadership of Eugene Leviné who refused Landauer's services. [20] Counterrevolutionary troops

---

20. For further discussion of the chaotic events that led to the establishment of the Bavarian

overthrew the Bavarian Soviet at the end of April. On May 1, 1919, Landauer was arrested and murdered the next day.[21]

II. The Philosophical Bases of Liberatarian Life

Derided as an anarchist and utopian socialist, Landauer, as his works immediately reveal, was an astute political thinker, an interesting philosophical mystic, a capable literary critic as well as a perceptive opponent of positivist science and an advocate of art as the expression of objective forms of knowledge][22] Interestingly, his insights into science and art foreshadow his idea of socialism and his criticisms of Second International Marxism. For Landauer, modern science at its best is simply a useful ensemble of predictive abstractions. The value of these abstract constructs lies not in their alleged exact explications of reality as such, nor in their rationalized conception of the world. Rather, scientific generalizations are valid *only* as tentative observations and partial operational instruments. Anticipating certain arguments of the Frankfurt School, Landauer describes modern science's actual function as an identity theory that presumes to describe reality fully, while in fact abstractly manipulating the objective world into total conformity with its formal conceptualizations.

In this regard, Landauer deepens Fritz Mauthner's linguistic critique of science, which portrays science as a richer, but by no means qualitatively superior, form of dealing with everyday sense data.[23] For Landauer and Mauthner, all forms of knowledge are essentially culturally-delimited sense data that individual thought captures in linguistic expressions; thus, the form and content of individual

Soviet, see Erich Eyck, *A History of the Weimar Republic*, Vol. 1 (New York, 1962), pp. 78-79; S. William Halperin, *Germany Tried Democracy* (New York, 1946), pp. 122-125; and Richard M. Watt, *The Kings Depart. The Tragedy of Germany: Versailles and the German Revolution* (New York, 1968), pp. 294-297, and pp. 325-341.

21. See Ernst Toller, *I Was a German* (London, 1934), pp. 244-245.

22. Here Landauer clearly anticipates many of the insights later made by Walter Benjamin and Theodor W. Adorno. See Martin Jay, *The Dialectical Imagination* (Boston, 1973), pp. 173-218, and Susan Buck-Morss, *The Origin of Negative Dialectics* (New York, 1977), pp. 122-135.

23. For a very exacting discussion of how Mauthner affected Landauer, see Maurer, *Call to Revolution*, pp. 48-76. Also see Allan Janik and Stephen Toulmin, *Wittgenstein's Vienna* (New York, 1973), for more discussion on Mauthner's general intellectual influence in turn-of-the-century German culture.

memory, collective culture, social history, or positive science are nothing more than the form and content of language and its metaphors.[24] Analytical abstractions, consequently, are individual projections used to understand the world, but these conceptual mediations—particularly the highly formalized abstractions of science that methodically restrict their own linguistic richness and metaphor—do not adequately grasp reality as such. Because all thought forms are arbitrary projections of historical traditions constituted by the language community's interaction with its sensual environs, Landauer sees scientific laws as necessarily failing to circumscribe the stuff of reality.

Although language does not provide a medium adequate to the claims of positivist science, it is nevertheless the most accurate human means for potentially understanding reality, because the metaphors of language can both project and retain the anthropomorphic constitution of the world. The real world of nature and society is knowable, but only through linguistic or artistic metaphors which base themselves in culturally projected sense data. Human will cannot alter the forms of human knowledge without abandoning the false mechanical concepts of science that impoverish human understanding by demanding the artificial maintenance of abstract, static and formal universals. Such (pure rationalism) leads to partial control of the external, objective world, but only at the cost of de-humanization and systematic misunderstanding of the human, interior, subjective world.

The growth of humanity depends, therefore, not on the progress of science but rather on the metaphorical mediations of art which can lead to a regeneration of social spirituality, of *Geist*. Here, however, Landauer's distance from the 1970s creates certain terminological difficulties, the clearest example of which is this concept of "spirit." It would be mistaken to understand Landauer as a traditional religious thinker and assume his use of "spirit" refers to a divine agency above humanity. Nor does the Hegelian spirit cast light on Landauer's term because of his radical rejection of the teleology intrinsic to Hegel's thought. A close approximation of Landauer's meaning would be "consciousness," but here too caution is called for. "Spirit" certainly

---

24. Maurer, pp. 60-64.

does not mean an arbitrarily defined consciousness, that is, *any* set of values and opinions. It also differs from the Marxist notion of consciousness as the superstructural reflection of the productive base. For Landauer, no material conditions necessitate particular forms of thought nor does he, as Marxism can, claim to speak from the standpoint of history's end, from which other deviating forms of consciousness are proclaimed to be false.

Landauer's spirit is instead a folk consciousness or a full consciousness, an inner individual awareness of social ties that demand cooperative activity. Except during historical periods of atomistic isolation, it is less a quality of individuals than an entire mode of existence for a society able to recognize itself as such. The absence of this consciousness is not merely ideology but rather social death. Organic social reciprocity is displaced, then, by forms of state domination to which the individual, no longer an active participant in the folk consciousness, is subordinated. For Landauer, folk consciousness was anything but the chauvinistic élan of nation-state worship that the right-wing *völkisch* movements touted in Wilhelmine Germany.[25] He saw the folk consciousness as the generic memory and historical essence of all a people's past ancestors imbedded deeply in the common language as well as in the psychic make-up of every individual formed in the cultural interaction of the group with its milieu.[26] Thus, spirit is the cornerstone of Landauer's anarchism, both as his notion of subjectivity and as his alternative to bureaucratic administration.

Hence, Landauer sees the folk as living communities of thought and experience which are not explicable in positivist scientific statements. Human essence resides in each individual as communal consciousness, or social individuality; personal individuality is formed within the linguistic-metaphorical content of the shared experience. Art, music, and poetry effectively can interpret this consciousness as a form of

---

25. Rather, as Eugene Lunn argues, Landauer represents a left-wing form of the *völkisch* current of thought. The turn of *völkisch* thought to the right is ultimately not indicative of the quality of such thought, but rather of the self-imposed constraints of the traditional Marxist left, which failed to appropriate the leftist potential of the *völkisch* movement.

26. The ultimate source of these notions is Johann Gottfried von Herder, especially his *Reflections on the Philosophy of the History of Mankind*, abridged with introduction by Frank E. Manuel (Chicago, 1968).

worldly understanding. Here, Landauer's life-long interest in poets of folk consciousness—Shakespeare in England, Whitman in the United States, or Hölderlin in Germany—illustrates his understanding of the folk spirit as well as each individual poet's artistry which articulates his social individuality. The poet, as in Whitman's "Song of Myself," speaks not for his *own* self, but for his *folk* self, embedded in his individual consciousness, his language, culture, society, and communal order. Thus, spirit corresponds to the pre-categorical and metatheoretical essence which is embodied in the artistic creations of poets and the communal praxis of socialists. Similarly, as Landauer asserts in *Skepsis und Mystik*, individuals must assume the spirit of their social individuality in activity because, "we have been satisfied until now to transform the universe into the human spirit, or better, into human intellect; let us now transform ourselves into universal spirit." [27]

It follows, then, that for Landauer socialism is the communal regeneration of the individual's inner essence through creative activity, familial love, and social labor. Socialism is not the socialization of the means of production under the dictatorship of the proletariat. On the contrary, "socialism is an endeavor to create a new reality with the help of an ideal." [28] Thus, wholly in keeping with Landauer's anarchist designs, such socialism can never come to pass through *state* action. In fact, the modern state is the negation of a former folk consciousness whose waning spirit was replaced after the Middle Ages with the state's laws, police, and prisons. The spiritual basis of socialism is already present in each individual as folk consciousness, but it will become an emancipatory collective subjectivity only if it is created by dedicated people working to transform themselves. Here, the socialist ideal set forth in *For Socialism* projects a prefigurative image of communal living that captures the essence of the full, folk consciousness practiced as a *social revolution*, "a peaceful building, an organizing in a new spirit and to a new spirit and nothing more." [29] These premises, in turn, prompted Landauer to break almost entirely with the working class as the historically determined agent of socialist revolution. In

27. Quoted in Maurer, p. 68.
28. *Ibid.*, p. 167.
29. *Ibid.*, p. 97.

fact, for Landauer, the de-humanization intrinsic to the forms of capitalist labor increasingly prevents the proletarians from becoming revolutionary as industrialization becomes more deeply rooted. Here, Landauer turns to "outsiders"—farmers, students, intellectuals, the surviving craftspeople, and small shopowners—to serve as the revolutionary agents of moral regeneration. Consequently, he recommends that small, agrarian communes be established as an opposition to modern capitalism. In such intimate communal settings, he maintains, the folk consciousness can reassert itself fully and provide the truly revolutionary foundations of a new culture, a new society, and a new community of communities free from the exploitation of the advanced capitalist state. "Socialism," then, "is the attempt to lead man's common life to a bond of common spirit in freedom, that is, to religion." [30]

III. The Anarcho-Socialist Critique of Marxism

Marxism, as the *scientific* expression of socialism, symbolizes the intrusion of the positive scientist's manipulative consciousness into the struggle for socialist community. For Landauer, Marxism is part of the problem posed by industrialization. As he suggests, "the father of Marxism is steam." In spite of Marxism's alleged objectivity and systematicity, Landauer considers it a repressive mystification used by "professors who want to rule." Indeed, as Landauer continues in *For Socialism*, "old wives prophesy from coffee dregs. Karl Marx prophesied from steam." As a significant political force, Marxism developed a popular following only in the 1890s and presented neither the exclusive nor the most articulate critique of modern industry. Only a banally amnesiac misreading of the past portrays Marxism or Marxism-Leninism as the sole heir to the legacy of nineteenth century working class struggle. What has been forgotten, or forcibly repressed, is that a wide range of tendencies, all offering opposition to aspects of capitalist industrialization, flourished during the period. In this sense, Landauer provides a cogent synthesis of Proudhon and Kropotkin, while highlighting the impossibility of an effective Marxist critique of capitalism. His arguments focus primarily on the central tenet of orthodox Marxism, namely, its own scientific character, i.e.,

30. Buber, *Paths in Utopia*, p. 55.

the ability to describe objective laws of development within capitalism that lead inexorably to socialism. This (teleological) view of history forced the social democrats, from Landauer's vantage, to applaud capitalist growth, for it was precisely that growth, that centralization, and that rationalization of the economy which would sooner or later blossom into socialism, regardless of whether the ballot box or a *coup d'état* ushered in the final phase of human maturation. Given this dogmatic faith in the inevitability of progress, social democracy was hardly in a position to articulate a fundamental critique of capitalist industrialization. Not only does Landauer jettison the sanguine trust in the beneficence of technology; he also renounces the objectivist teleology which is at the root of historical optimism.

Faith in progress coupled with materialist determinism debilitated the possibility of praxis within traditional Marxism. Inevitability displaced activism. A stop-gap measure was provided in democratic centralism by which the question of praxis was subordinated to acceptance of the party, but only at the cost of intellectual capitulation. Landauer, on the other hand, rescued the possibility of action in the present by lifting the weight of a rigid *telos* from the socialists's shoulders. Socialism is not inevitable, he argued, but it could come if it were created. Similarly, no material base, no measure of industrial progress, no matter how great, could guarantee an end to history; but a socio-cultural movement concerned with socialist forms of living is possible everywhere and at all times. The subordination of the present to a promised land in the future could only spell defeat for the emancipatory forces. In *For Socialism*, this self-defeating teleology is presented as a cornerstone of the Marxist structure. Thus, Marxism, despite its revolutionary appearance, functions in fact as an impediment to socialism; or, as Landauer continually reaffirms, "Marxism...is the plague of our age and the curse of the socialist movement." [31]

In the light of Landauer's critique, nineteenth century scientific socialism ceases to appear as a radical critique of the *status quo*. Rather, behind its revolutionary pretenses, it buttresses the development of capitalist structures. Furthermore, the orthodox

---

31. Lunn, p. 201.

Marxism of social democracy mimics the practices of the oppressive regime that it seeks to destroy. [It too sacrifices immediate experience in the present at the altar of progress understood as the expansion of administrative control.] In discarding this teleological structure, then, Landauer was forced to articulate a concept of socialism independent of both historical determinism and the organizational authoritarianism that it engendered.

For Landauer, socialism was no longer a matter of history's endpoint, but rather a cultural movement, possible but never inevitable in the present. It meant overcoming the atomistic individualism which had been gnawing at the heart of European society for four centuries. It entailed the conscious decision to act socially. No god, and no scientifically-determined *telos* would redeem a mankind unwilling to redeem itself. In highlighting the voluntary character of political praxis, Landauer underscores his commitment to existential subjectivity, vindicating it against the objectivist dialectic of nature characteristic of an earlier materialism. To the extent that he describes the organization of socialist society, it is by no means one in which a planning agency dominates the various parts. On the contrary, he calls for a decentralized, communal arrangement that could encourage active participation without necessitating total integration. Any political movement that attempted a total integration of its members into an objectively defined correct consciousness, like the SPD, could only conclude its project in an authoritarian collectivism.

To be sure, as soon as the SPD resumed its legitimate political activities in Germany with the lapse of the anti-socialist legislation of 1878-1890,[32] it immediately reinforced its commitment to Marxism in the new Erfurt Program.[33] Yet, even as it reformed its ranks, many of its members resisted its all too obvious organizational authoritarianism under its political "drillmaster," August Bebel.[34] The anarchists, in particular, who had disrupted the founding sessions of the Second

---

32. Joll, p. 64.
33. See Carl Schorske, *German Social Democracy 1905-1917* (New York, 1972), pp. 3-6.
34. Indeed, Bebel was legendary for never passing up an opportunity to compare his organizational creation, the German Social Democratic Party, to that other "great" German organizatonal achievement—the Prussian army.

International in Paris during 1889,[35] and the anarcho-socialists who emerged from the Jungen movement, seriously challenged the party's essentially state-like operations. Hence, they promptly were expelled at the party congress in Erfurt in 1891.[36] Initially, the Jungen merely criticized the unrevolutionary methods of SPD parliamentarianism, while affirming the use of parliamentary tactics to demonstrate working class intransigence and revolutionary spirit. Their personal attacks on the party leadership for sapping the party's revolutionary purpose, however, led to their immediate expulsion. This reaction by the SPD executive, in turn, nurtured the Jungen critique of the SPD as an authoritarian party-state acting out political tyranny within its working class organization while hiding behind its mask of Marxist revolutionary theory.[37] By early as 1893, Landauer had witnessed this official social democratic repression of both anarchist activists and spontaneous proletarian unrest, and he was able to draw the conclusion that the party's subordination of the present to a socialism in the future only spelled defeat for the emancipatory forces.

The Jungen and the anarcho-socialists, then, posed a basic challenge to the SPD's designs for building a socialist society. Initially, the anarchist presence in the SPD called into question the legitimacy of the SPD in the eyes of the ruling authorities, who crudely regarded all anarchists as "propagandists of the deed" intent upon bombing and assassination.[38] Although the threat of renewed repression by the state was constantly on the minds of the SPD executive, it was the anarchists' attacks on the SPD's ideology and tactics that represented a more fundamental challenge both to its own success as well as the success of the Second International, which the SPD dominated.[39] With regard to its ideology, most anarchists agreed with Landauer's characterization of official Marxism as a rationale to mask the political

---

35. See Joll, pp. 30-48.

36. *Ibid.,* p. 64.

37. As Eugene Lunn notes, p. 70, much of the Jungen critique later was adopted by Robert Michels in his 1915 work, *Political Parties.*

38. In fact, the anarchists were so effective in their assassinations that Kaiser Wilhelm II seriously pressed the reintroduction of anti-socialist legislation in 1894. See Joll, pp. 56-58.

39. To be sure, it was the domination of the German Social Democratic Party in the Second International that led George Bernard Shaw to quip after the 1896 London Congress that, "An International Congress that everybody laughs at and nobody fears is a gratifying step in advance." Quoted in Joll, p. 75.

subordination of the working classes. Unwilling to accept Karl Kautsky's orthodox Marxist predictions, the anarchists questioned the Erfurt Program and continually pushed the SPD toward "revolution-making" strategies rather than submitting to its reformist liberal tactics that Kautsky considered "revolutionary" at heart. While the anarchists continued to point out the increasing contradictions between the party's Marxist science and the actual course of political reality, the SPD grew even more repressive as an organization. By 1896, the anarchists were successfully ousted from the International, largely as a result of the SPD's maneuvering, and they never again posed a serious internal threat to social democracy's bureaucratic authoritarianism.

Landauer's insights become even more interesting when juxtaposed with the revisionism debates that racked the SPD at the turn of the century. As he had foreseen, when confronted by the liberalizing elements of Bernstein's anti-Marxist critiques, the SPD dogmatically rededicated itself to the Marxist ideology in order to maintain the "revolutionary" character of the party's challenge to the established order. Yet, given the fact that Marxism failed to account for Germany's and Europe's rising economic prosperity, the ideology simply served as the legitimation of political conformity with the SPD's continued orthodoxy in both Germany and the International.

Sensing this dogmatism, Bernstein almost totally rejected the orthodox analysis of Kautsky's Erfurt Program. According to its principles, Marx's theoretical analysis of capitalist crisis was wholly supported by the historical developments at the turn of the century. Bernstein ardently challenged these tenets and suggested instead that wealth was not becoming centralized, that class conflict was not mounting, and that economic misery was not spreading among the working classes.[40] On the contrary, the business cycle was becoming normalized; hence, class conflict was lessening in the general extension of economic well-being. Thus, he called for increasing acceptance of liberal policies: anti-protectionism, greater democratization, free trade, and peaceful settlement of international conflict.

---

40. See Eduard Bernstein, *Evolutionary Socialism: A Criticism and Affirmation* (New York, 1961).

In doing so, however, he also advocated less dependence upon Marxist science, a position that led, in turn, to greater reliance upon neo-Kantian ethics as an intellectual legitimation for divorcing theory and politics, science and ethics. Bernstein accordingly emphasized freedom in action as a result of an autonomous ethical decision, whereas Kautsky and the SPD directorate clung more closely to the causal determinations of party science to orient their political practice. Weakly paralleling Landauer, Bernstein also held that socialism was not inevitable, but that it was instead an ethical ideal: "something that ought to be, or a movement towards something that ought to be."[41] As they had also reacted to the anarchists' voluntarism, Kautsky and the SPD ridiculed Bernstein's ethical voluntarism as an unscientific reversion to pre-Marxian practices. For the SPD, historical necessity maintained its hold on bourgeois society and demanded renewed working class intransigence to deal with the unexpected economic upturn. To them socialism was not simply an extension of liberal reformist logic as it apparently was to Bernstein, but instead represented a new historical moment demanding the constitution of new knowledge and a new morality possible only in a mass working class party which would effectively blend, in Kautsky's analysis, theory and practice.

Plainly, the debate ended in deadlock and led to theoretical catastrophe for both factions. Kautsky, in reaction to Bernstein's neo-Kantian liberal idealism, was driven even further into his Darwinistic materialist evolutionism. This crude scientistic naturalism ultimately concluded in the denial of philosophy itself. On the other hand, Bernstein's neo-Kantian divorce of theory and practice progressively identified the "socialist" ideal and the ethical freedom of the working classes as liberal politics and laborite social reformism, which failed to transcend the immediacy of everyday parliamentary politics. For the SPD organization, Bernstein's formula for gradual change and reform appeared quite ridiculous, as the transition to socialism necessarily required a sharp break into a new stage of history and a new class alliance that Bernstein failed to accept in his

---

41. George Lichtheim, *Marxism: An Historical and Critical Study*, revised edition (New York, 1965), p. 296.

theoretical pronouncements. Here, Landauer's transitional strategy challenges both the orthodox and the revisionist as he argues for spiritual transformation through communal prefiguration of the future in present activity.

As Landauer also argued, the SPD orthodoxy remained hampered by its philosophy of history. By casting historical development as a deterministic casual chain, it left little discretion to human ethical will. Yet, as both Bernstein and Landauer maintained, even if the party's Marxist science *did* "prove" socialism to be historical necessity, it failed to demonstrate its moral basis or its ethical superiority as a form of human emancipation. Landauer, in contradistinction to both the orthodox Marxist and the revisionist, addresses himself almost exclusively to precisely this task of concretizing the ethical desirability of socialism, while refuting and rebuking the materialism of the International.

IV. *Landauer's Legacy*

These debates within the Second International as well as the themes typical of the *fin-de-siècle* cultural crisis provide the background; they explain the genesis of Landauer's work. As he explicitly underscores in the preface to the 1919 edition, his criticism represented a response to the failures of the various Marxist currents — including both traditional social democracy and the Bolshevik alternative [42] — a response which however transcended the limits of the discussion within the organized working class movement in order to confront the disorder of Germany's socio-cultural situation. The needs and desires at the bottom of the widespread turbulent opposition to industrial capitalist society were not treated adequately by the programs of the Marxist orthodoxies. Precisely this failure of the German left allowed the political right to appropriate the general dissatisfaction that characterized German society. Of course, the right misused the issues with glaring contradictions between its ideological pronouncements, designed for mass appeal, and its actual policies, which only reinforced the modernizing tendencies. Indeed, for all its glorification of nature, the right would only construct modern highways and

---

42. See Pross, p. 530.

sophisticated war-machines. Invoking autonomy and independence, it strengthened bureaucratic hierarchy and state interventionism. Finally, its paeans to the provincial virtues, aimed at the anti-urban, anti-Berlin mood, only hid a more rigorous integration of the state and local administrations into the centralized organization. The subrational mouthing of shibboleth-like community (*Gemeinschaft*) only heightened the isolation and the impotence of the individual in society. This was the fascist reality that openly contradicted the successful fascist appropriation of tradition and of broadly-based dissatisfaction with the course of advanced industrial development. The cultural victory of the right was the outcome of the left's inability to speak to this malaise, except in pedantic, uncomprehending tones. In this sense, Landauer's critique of Marxism foreshadows the attempts to develop theories of fascism in the twenties and thirties by figures such as August Thalheimer, Ernst Bloch, Wilhelm Reich and Franz Neumann, who were dissatisfied with the platitudes of the Comintern.[43] Landauer's insights, however, had raised similar questions two decades earlier.

Thus, *For Socialism* transcends the specific context of the turn of the century milieu by anticipating the themes raised by various generations of Western Marxists and radical thinkers throughout the twentieth century. Landauer is the missing link between the oppositional forces of the late nineteenth century and the work of Lukács, Korsch and Gramsci as well as the critical theory of Benjamin, Adorno and Horkheimer. Despite his vague, quasi-expressionist style, it would be erroneous to relegate him to the level of a mere precursor of these later thinkers. On the contrary, a radicalism characterizes *For Socialism* that is much more profound than that of later works anxious to salvage certain aspects of Marxism, which Landauer already was prepared to reject wholly. In fact, given Lukács' explicitly Hegelianized Marxism that leads straight into a defense of democratic centralism or Adorno's implicit teleology with its

43. See Niels Kadritzke, *Faschismus und Krise: Zum Verhältnis von Politik und Oekonomie im Nationalsozialismus* (Frankfurt am Main, 1976), especially pp. 17-92; Anson Rabinbach, "Ernst Bloch's *Heritage of Our Times* and Fascism," *New German Critique* 11 (Spring 1977), pp. 5-21; and Reinhard Kühnl, ed., *Texte zur Faschismusdiskussion I: Positionen und Kontroversen* (Reinbeck bei Hamburg, 1974), pp. 8-9.

concomitant despair, nowhere is the problem of subjectivist praxis as important as it is in Landauer's work.

Landauer anticipates critical theory, while also serving as witness to the gound lost during half a century of subterranean orthodoxy within the left-wing of Western Marxism. He also proves quite relevant to the present as the last vestiges of New Left subjectivism are disappearing beneath a rising tide of scientific socialism. Republishing *For Socialism* provides a new perspective on the history of the Second International, which is all too often understood only as a prelude to Lenin. At the same time, Landauer's study raises issues which effectively question today's neo-orthodoxy at a fundamental level. While radical claims that a profound social transformation is inevitable today only can be attributed to a blind romanticism numb to a history of defeats, Landauer upholds an image of change that becomes possible only through collective action, personal participation, and a large measure of faith in the present.

FOREWORD
TO
THE SECOND EDITION

The revolution has come, though I did not expect it this way. War has come, just as I expected; and in that war I soon saw defeat and revolution relentlessly approaching.

With a truly profound bitterness I state: it is now clear that I was essentially correct in this *Call for Socialism* and in articles in my journal *The Socialist*. A political revolution in Germany had not yet occured; now it has been completed, and only the revolutionaries' inability to construct the new economy, in particular, as well as the new freedom and self-determination, could be held responsible if a re-action should bring about the reestablishment of new privileged powers. All shades of Marxist Social Democratic parties, in all their varieties, are incapable of political practice, of the constitution of humanity and its popular institutions and of establishing a government representing labor and peace, just as they cannot attain a theoretical comprehension of the social facts, as they most horribly demonstrated before, during and after the war, from Germany to Russia, from their militaristic enthusiasm to their unspiritual and uncreative reign of terror, which are essentially related and were very curiously allied. However, if it is true, as suggested both by some news reports and our hope's trembling desire for grace and a miracle, that Russian Bolsheviks, by a similarly beautiful and even more transforming growth than was displayed by Friedrich Adler in Austria and Kurt Eisner in Germany, have risen above themselves, their theoretical dogmatism and barren practice, and given federation and freedom priority over centralism and military-proletarian authoritarian organization, that they have become creative and have overcome the industrial proletarian and the professor of death in them by the spirit of the Russian peasant, the spirit of Tolstoy, by the one eternal spirit, then that truly is not due to Marxism but rather to the heavenly spirit of the revolution, which under the firm grip and rapid catapult of necessity, reveals buried strata in man's psyche, [especially that of the Russian man's], and opens up secret wellsprings of subconscious strength.

Capitalism, furthermore, has not displayed the anticipated progressiveness of slowly and peacefully transforming itself into socialism; nor has it produced socialism by a miraculous sudden collapse. And how could the principle of evil, oppression, robbery, and philistine routine be expected to perform miracles? In these times when routine has become a malignant scourge, it is spirit that must lead to revolution, spirit that performs miracles; thus overnight it changed the constitution of the German Reich, reducing a governmental structure, which German professors had considered inviolably sacred, into a past episode of the German landed and industrial Junkers. The government has collapsed; socialism is the only salvation. It certainly did not result as a blossom of capitalism; it is the heir and repudiated son waiting at the door behind which the corpse of his unnatural father rots. Nor can socialism be added to the beautiful body of society as an apex of national wealth and a sumptuous economy; it must be created almost out of nothing amid chaos. In despair I called for socialism; but out of that despair I drew great hope and joyous resolution, and the despair which I and the likes of me bore in our hearts has not become a permanent condition. May those who must now begin the work of construction not lack hope, a desire to work, knowledge, and an enduring creativity.

Everything said here about the collapse applied fully only to Germany at present and to the nations which, voluntarily or not, have shared its fate. As was said, not capitalism as such has collapsed by virtue of its immanent impossibility, but the capitalism of one group of nations, acting in conjunction with autocracy and militarism, has been ruined by the liberally administered capitalism of another, militarily weaker, capitalistically stronger area, in final conjunction with the volcanic eruption of popular rage of its own people. I will not predict when and in what form the collapse of the other, more clever representative of capitalism and imperialism will occur. The social causes necessary for any revolution to take place are present everywhere. However, the need for political liberation, the only reason for a revolution to move toward a goal and become more than a revolt, is of varying strength in those countries which have experienced democratic political revolutions. The following seems to be evident: the more free political mobility exists in a country, and the greater the adaptability of government institutions to democracy, the more terrible and unproductive, however, the struggle will be when social hardship, injustice and degradation finally generate the phantom of a revolution and, consequently an all-too-real civil war, if steps are not taken to establish socialism immediately. The symptoms, which first appeared in Switzerland—in ugly combination with war, war-profiteering, Swiss war-*ersatz* and non-Swiss war-corruption—are clear enough to anyone who can distinguish creative work from haplessly cruel excesses and spasmodic savagery.

For the revolution can only be a political one. It would not gain the support of the enslaved masses, if they did not also desire to break free of social oppression and economic hardship. However, the transformation of social institutions, of property relations, of the type of economy cannot come by way of revolution. In these matters, action from below can only shake off, destroy and abandon something; action from above, even by a revolutionary government, can only abolish and command, whereas socialism must be built, erected, organized out of a new spirit. This new spirit prevails mightily and ardently in the revolution. Robots become men. Cold, unimaginative men are fired with enthusiasm. The entire *status quo*, including opinions, positive and negative, is cast into doubt. Reason, which formerly focused only on selfish interest, becomes rational thinking and thousands of men sit or pace restlessly in their rooms, for the first time in their lives forging plans for the common welfare. Everything becomes accessible to the good. The incredible miracle is brought into the realm of possibility. The reality which is otherwise hidden in our souls, in the structures and rhythms of art, in the faith-structures of religion, in dream and love, in dancing limbs and gleaming glances, now presses for fulfillment. However, the tremendous danger remains that the old humdrum way and empty imitation will take hold of the revolutionaries and make them shallow, uncultured radicals, with the ringing rhetoric and violent gestures, who neither know, nor want to know, that the transformation of society can come only in love, work, and silence.

They also ignore another point, despite the experiences of past revolutions. All these revolutions were a great renewal, a bubbling refreshment, a high point of nations; but their permanent results were slight. Ultimately they brought a change only in the forms of political disenfranchisement. [Political freedom, maturity, honest pride, self-determination and an organic, corporative coherence of the masses out of one unifying spirit, voluntary associations in public life—this can only be achieved by a great adjustment, by economic and social justice, by socialism.]How could there be a commonwealth of true communities in our era, in which Christianity affirms the equality of all the children of men, in origin, rights and destiny; how could there be a free public life, pervaded by the all-fulfilling, dynamic spirit of enthusiastically progressive men and deep, strong women, if slavery, disinheritance and ostracism persist in any form and guise?

The political revolution which brings the spirit to power and makes it the strong imperative and decisive implementation, can clear the way for socialism, for a change of conditions by a renewed spirit. But decrees can, at most, incorporate men as government slaves into a new military-like economy; the new spirit of justice must create its own forms of economy. The idea must embrace the needs of the moment within its long-range view and shape them energetically. What was previously only an ideal, is realized by the work of renewal born out of the revolution.

The need for socialism is there. Capitalism is collapsing. It no longer works. The fiction that capital works has burst like a bubble; the only thing that attracted the capitalist to his sort of work, to the risk of his fortune and the leadership and administration of enterprise, namely profit, no longer attracts him. The age of the profitability of capital, of interest and usury, is over; the mad war-profits were a dance of death. If we are not to perish in our Germany, to perish really and literally, the only salvation is work, real work done, performed and organized by an unselfish, fraternal spirit. New forms of work must be developed, freed from a tribute payable to capital, ceaselessly creating new values and new realities, harvesting and transforming the products of nature for human needs. The age of the productivity of labor is beginning; otherwise we have reached the end of the line.

Technology has placed both long known and newly discovered natural forces at man's service. The more people cultivate the earth and transform its products, the richer the harvest. Mankind can live in dignity and without care. No one need be another's slave, no one need be excluded and disinherited. Work, the means of life, need not become an arduous torment. All can live in openness to spirit, soul, play, and God. Revolutions and their painfully long, oppressive pre-history teach us that only the most extreme distress, only the feeling of sheer desperation brings the masses of men to reason, to the reason which, for wise men and children, always comes naturally; what horrors, ruins, hardships, scourges, plagues, conflagrations and wild cruelties are we to expect, if even at this fateful hour, reason, socialism, spiritual leadership and conformity to the spirit do not enter into men's minds?

Capital, which has been the parasitic master, must become the servant — but a form of capital that represents community, reciprocity, equality of exchange. O suffering men, are you still standing helplessly before the obvious and childishly easy solution? Even in this hour of need, that also was your hour of political action? Do you still remain animals that have lost their instincts and are stupified by reason, since you wait so long? Do you not yet see the error that lies in your boastful arrogance and indolence of heart? What has to be done is so clear and simple that every child understands it. The means are there; whoever looks around, sees it. The imperative of the spirit which leads the revolution can help us through great measures and undertakings. Submit to this spirit; petty interests must not hamper it. But its full implementation is impeded by heaps of rubble that have been piled upon the conditions and even the souls of the masses. One road is open, more open than ever, to help bring about revolution and the collapse of the present system: to begin on a small scale, and voluntarily, immediately, on all sides, *you* are called, you and your friends!

Otherwise the end is here: capital is losing its return due to economic conditions, governmental demands, and international obligations; a nation's indebtedness to other nations and to itself is expressed in finance policy by ever more debts. France, at the time of the great revolution, made a marvelous recovery from the debts of the *ancien régime* and its own financial turmoil by the great adjustment that began with the distribution of lands and the joy in work and enterprise unleashed by the liberation from bondage. Our revolution can and should distribute lands on a grand scale. It can and should create a new and revitalized farm population, but it certainly cannot give the capitalist class joy in work and enterprise. For capitalists, the revolution is only the end of the war: collapse and ruin. The capitalists, their industrial managers and their dealers lose not only their income but also will lose their raw materials and world market. Moreover, the negative component of socialism is there and no power can remove it from the earth: the complete, hourly increasing disinclination of the workers, indeed their psychic inability to continue to hire themselves out under capitalist conditions.

Socialism, then, must be built; it must be set into operation amid the collapse, in conditions of distress, crisis, improvisations. I will now shout from the rooftops how out of the greatest need the greatest virtue must be established, and the new labor corporations out of the fall of capitalism and the pressing needs of the living masses. I will not fail to rebuke the proletarians of industry, who consider themselves the only workers, for their narrow-mindedness, the wild obstinacy, intransigence and crudeness of their intellectual and emotional life, their irresponsibility and incapacity for a positive economic organization and leadership of enterprises. By absolving men of guilt and declaring them creatures of social conditions, one does not make these products of society different than they are, while the new world will be built not with men's causes but with the men themselves. I will delay to call upon government and municipal officials, leaders of cooperatives and large factories, technical and commercial employees and directors, lawyers, and officers whose roles in the present system will become superfluous, to help this movement, modestly, expertly and zealously, in a spirit of community and of personal originality. I will sharply criticize the government's counterfeiting of paper money that now goes by the name of monetary policy and especially the compensation for unemployment that is made in this so-called money, though every healthy person, no matter what profession he previously practiced, must participate in the construction of the new economy, in saving society from the greatest danger, when as much as possible has to be constructed and planned as possible. I will recommend the use of the presently unproductive military bureaucracy so that capitalism's unemployed can be led to positions where emergency economics, which must bring salvation, needs them; I will call for the strongest revolutionary energy, which will lead to the salvation and socialization of reality. At this point let me give a brief preliminary summary: what I have repeated again and again in the call which follows and in essays in my *Socialist*, which complement it, is that socialism is possible and necessary in every form of economy and technology. It has no use for the industrial and mercantile technology of capitalism nor for the mentality that produced this monstrosity. Because socialism must commence and because the realization of spirit and virtue is never mass-like and normal but rather results only from the self-sacrifice of the few and the new venture of pioneers, socialism must free itself from ruin out of poverty and joy in work. For its sake we must return to rural living and to a unification of industry, craftsmanship and agriculture, to save ourselves and learn justice and community. What Peter Kropotkin taught us about the methods of intensive soil cultivation and unification of intellectual and manual labor in his important and now famous book *The Field, the Factory, the Workshop* as well as the new form of credit and monetary cooperative must all be tested now in our most drastic need and with creative pleasure. Necessity demands, voluntarily but under threat of famine, a new start and construction, without which we are lost.

Let me add one last word, the most serious one. If we convert the greatest hardship into the greatest virtue and transform the emergency labor made necessary by the crisis into the provisional beginning of socialism, our humiliation will be credited to our honor. Let us disregard the question as to how our socialist republic, arising out of defeat and ruin, will stand among the victorious nations and the mighty countries presently devoted to capitalism. Let us not beg, let us fear nothing, let us not flinch. Let us act among the nations, like Job activated by his suffering, abandoned by God and the world in order to serve God and the world. Let us construct our economy and the institutions of our society so that we can rejoice in hard work and a worthy life. One thing is certain: when things go well with us in poverty, when our souls are glad, poor and honorable men in all other nations, in all of them will follow our example. Nothing, nothing in the world has such irresistible power of conquest as goodness does. We were politically retarded, were the most arrogant and provoking lackeys; the harm that resulted for us with the inevitability of destiny has incensed us against our masters, moved us to revolution. So at one stroke, namely the blow that struck us, we assumed leadership. We are to lead the way to socialism; how else could we lead than through our example? Chaos is here. New activities and turmoil are on the horizon. Minds are awakening, souls rising to responsibility, hands taking action. May the revolution bring rebirth. May, since we need nothing so much as new, uncorrupted men rising up out of the unknown darkness and depths, may these renewers, purifiers, saviors not be lacking to our nation. Long live the revolution, and may it grow and rise to new levels in hard, wonderful years. May the nations be imbued with the new, creative spirit out of their task, out of the new conditions, out of the primeval, eternal and unconditional depths, the new spirit that really does create new conditions. May the revolution produce religion, a religion of action, life, love, that makes men happy, redeems them and overcomes impossible situations. What does life matter? We will die soon, we all die, we do not live at all. Nothing lives but what we make of ourselves, what we do with ourselves. Creation lives; not the creature, only the creator. Nothing lives but the action of honest hands and the governance of a pure, genuine spirit.

Munich, January 3, 1919

Gustav Landauer

PREFACE
TO
THE FIRST EDITION

In my book *The Revolution* (Frankfurt a.M., 1907) I said: "Here is where our road leads: that such men as have gained insight and realized that it is impossble to continue living this way, have started uniting in associations and placing their labor in the service of their consumption. They will soon reach the limits set for them by the state; they lack a legal basis. This is the point where the revolution of which we have spoken till now goes further into a revolution of which nothing can be said, because it is still far off. Nor can anything be said here of social regeneration, of which only hints could be given. How one evaluates the beginnings and movements that now exist depends on what one expects in the future. I intend to continue this line of argument in another book and to treat the coming of socialism in context."

Since I still cannot manage to write the book promised by these lines, let the reader temporarily accept the following lecture without however forgetting that it is a lecture and claims to be nothing else. In such a lecture much must be said briefly and an emotional tone often must replace detailed argumentation; the flow of speech wants to move on. Let the reader take advantage of its being a printed lecture and reflect that many of the sentences in it could require a book for their proof and complete delineation. Let the reader sometimes set aside the lecture in order to reflect for himself on the particular subject, for perhaps then he will discover that what is said quickly need not lack reflection and basis.

I have chosen the form of a lecture because one of the tasks of language will always be to call others to oneself and because that was precisely my intention. Of course I speak differently here than I would before an assembly; I speak before the broad, indeterminate circle which the lonely man sees before his eyes in nocturnal work hours.

When I first gave this lecture—on May 26 and June 14—I summarized the content at the end of the second session in the "Twelve Articles of the Socialist League," which are printed at the end of the first edition. This marked the founding of the Socialist League, and its first members were enrolled already at that assembly. Soon the first group was founded; the "Work"-group in Berlin. At this moment there exist in Germany and Switzerland nineteen expressly constituted and a larger number of unnamed groups. Early in 1909 appeared the biweekly periodical *The Socialist*, in which I and others pursue our ideas further and seek to demonstrate their validity in the conditions and events of the nations, in the life of communities, families, individuals.

In addition we have until now published three pamphlets, which appeared in one volume together with a report on the previous activities of the League.

Hermsdorf, near Berlin, March 1911.

FOR SOCIALISM

by Gustav Landauer

1.

Whoever calls for socialism must be of the opinion that socialism is something that is either almost or fully absent, that is either not yet or no longer existent. One could object: "Of course, socialism, the socialist society, does not exist. It is not yet here, but efforts are being made to achieve it—insights, knowledge, teachings as to how it will come." No, the socialism I am calling for here is not meant so. Rather, by socialism I mean a tendency of the human will and an insight into conditions and ways that lead to its accomplishment. Yet this socialism hardly exists, and as miserably as ever. Therefore I speak to each one who wants to hear me, and I hope that my voice will finally reach very many who do not want to hear me; I call for socialism.

What is socialism? What do men mean by the word? And what is it that goes by the name of socialism today? Under what conditions, at what moment of society—of development, as is generally said—can it become reality?

Socialism is a striving, with the help of an ideal, to create a new reality. This first attempt is necessary even though the word "ideal" has fallen into disrepute due to pitiful hypocrites and base weaklings who like to go by the name of idealists and to uncultured drudges of science who like to call themselves realists. In unspiritual times of decline, un-culture, un-spirit, and misery, men who suffer not only externally but also internally under this general condition which seeks to engulf them fully—in their life, thought, feeling and will—men who resist this engulfment must have an ideal. They have an insight into the oppressive depravity and debasement of their situation. They are unspeakably disgusted with the misery that surrounds them like a swamp. They have energy that presses forward and longs for something better, and thus arises in them, an image of a pure, salutary, joyous mode of human communality in lofty beauty and perfection. They see in broad, general lines how it could be if a group, no matter how big or small, wanted and acted accordingly; if an entire country or countries ardently grasped this new idea and exerted their influence to bring it about. And now they no longer say: it can be so. Instead, they say: it should, and must come about. Once they grasp the prior history of human generations, they do not say: this ideal must become reality, as plainly and explicitly, as it stands on paper. They know well: the ideal is the ultimate in beauty and joy of life, the best thing their mind and spirit can imagine. It is a portion of spirit, reason and thought. However reality is never identical with the thinking of individual men. It would be boring if it were so, and we, consequently, had a duplicated world: first, in the anticipatory idea, second, in exact facsimile in the external world. It has never been so, and it will never be so. The ideal does not become reality; but our reality is realized in our time through the ideal, only through the ideal. We envisage something beyond which we see no better possibility. We perceive the ultimate and say: "That is what I want! "—and then we do everything to achieve it. The individual, overcome as if by illumination, seeks companions and finds them. There are others, into whose minds and hearts the idea has come like a flash of lightning and a storm. It is something in the air for the likes of them. Furthermore he finds others who were only sleeping lightly, whose understanding was covered only by a thin membrane and whose energy lay only under a mild anaesthetic. They are now together. They seek ways together. They hold discussions in small groups and with the masses, in the big cities, in smaller cities, and in the country. External distress awakens internal distress. Sacred dissatisfaction is aroused and stimulated; something like a spirit—spirit is communal spirit, spirit is union and freedom, spirit is an association of men, soon we will see it even more clearly—a spirit is coming over men; and where the spirit is present stands the people, and where the people are, there is a forward-driving wedge, a will. Where there is a will, there is a way. This word is true; but the way is only there. And the light becomes ever clearer, penetrates ever deeper. The veil, net, dull swampy mist is raised ever higher. A people unites, awakens. Actions are done. Supposed obstacles are recognized as insignificant and easily surmounted. Other obstacles are removed with united strength, for spirit is joy, power, movement, which nothing on earth can impede. This is the point I am trying to make! This voice and this uncontrollable longing burst forth out of the hearts of the individuals in an equal and unified way; and so this new reality is created. It will, of course, be different from the ideal, similar to it, but not identical. It will be better, for it is no longer a dream of intuitive, desirous and pained men, but rather a life, a communality, a social life of living men. It will be a people; it will be culture, joy. Who knows today what joy is? The lover when he contemplates his beloved with the feeling, indistinct or clear, that she is the quintessence of all that is life and creates life; the creative artist in a rare hour alone with a friend of like mind, or when in his mind and in his work he anticipates the beauty and fullness which will one day become alive in the people; the prophetic spirit who hastens ahead of centuries and is sure of eternity. Who else knows joy today, who knows what complete, great, rapturous joy is? Nobody today; nobody, for a long time. In some eras entire peoples were seized and motivated by a spirit of joy. They were so in the times of revolution, but there was not sufficient clarity in their exhilaration. There was too much dark smoldering in their ardour. They wanted something but they did not know what. And the ambitious politicians, advocates, representatives of special interests ruined everything again, while mindless greed and ambition swept away what sought to prepare the ground for the spirit to grow into a people. We have such advocates today, even if they do not go by that name. We have them and they have a hold on us. We have been warned, warned by history.

2.

Socialism is the tendency of will of united persons to create something new for the sake of an ideal.

So let us see what the old system is, and what previous reality was like, in our era. Not our time in the limited sense of now, a few years or a few decades; rather our own time as at the very least the past four hundred years.

For let us impress it on our minds and let us state it here at the beginning: socialism is a great cause with far-reaching consequences. It wishes to help lead declining families of men back to the height of a blossoming culture, to spirit and thus to unity and freedom.

Such words grate on the ears of professors and pamphleteers and they also displease those whose thinking is impregnated by these corrupters, who promulgate the doctrine that men, and also animals, plants and the whole world, are undergoing constant progress, in an upward movement from the very lowest level to the very highest; on and on, from the deepest filth of hell to the highest heavens. And so absolutism, serfdom, mercenariness, capitalism, hardship and degeneracy, all these things are supposed to be only progressive steps and stages on the road to socialism. We adhere to no such so-called scientific illusions. We see the world and human history completely differently. We say it differently.

We say that nations have their golden ages, the high points of their culture, and that they descend again from these pinnacles. We say that our people of Europe and America have been such declining nations for a long time — approximately since the discovery of America.

Nations reach their periods of greatness and maintain them when they are dominated by one spirit. That too sounds bad to the ears of those who call themselves socialists nowadays although they are not; we have just caught a glimpse of them in their Darwinistic garb, these adherents of the so-called materialistic conception of history. This will be treated below, and for the moment we must go on. We will meet Marxism again on our way and we will stop it and say to its face what it is: the plague of our times and the curse of the socialist movement!

It is the spirit — the spirit of thinkers, the spirit of men overpowered by emotion, of great sufferers, the spirit of those whose self-awareness and love coalesce in a great knowledge of the world — it is spirit which has led the nations to greatness, unity and freedom. Out of the individuals erupted a compelling matter-of-fact necessity to unite in common endeavor with their human brothers. Then the society of societies was there, communality based on voluntary association.

How did man, someone will probably ask, attain this intelligence and insight to abandon his isolation and to join with his compatriots first in smaller, then in larger groups?

The question is stupid and can only be asked by professors of declining times. For society is as old as man; it is the first, given fact. Wherever men have been, they were joined in hordes, clans, tribes and guilds. They migrated, lived and worked together. They were individual men held together by a common spirit, which is a natural and not extrinsically imposed compulsion (even what is called instinct in the animals is a common spirit).

But this natural compulsion of the unifying quality and common spirit, until now in known human history, has always needed external forms: religious symbols and cults, ideas of faith, prayer rituals or things of this sort.

Therefore spirit is in the nations always connected with unspirit, and deep symbolic thinking with superstitious opinion. The warmth and love of the unifying spirit is overshadowed by the stiff coldness of dogma. Truth, arising from such depths that it can be expressed only in imagery, is replaced by the nonsense of literalness.

This is followed by external organization. The church and the secular organizations of external coercion gain strength and grow continually worse: serfdom, feudalism, the various departments and authorities, the state.

This leads to an eventual decline of spirit among and over the people, and of the immediacy that flows from the individuals and leads them to unity. The spirit withdraws into individuals. It was inwardly strong individuals, representatives of the people, who had carried the spirit to the people; now it lives within the individuals, ingenious men who are consumed in all their might, but are without a people: isolated thinkers, poets, and artists without a social contest, without eternal roots, almost as if hovering in the air. Sometimes the spirit seizes them as if out of a dream of ancient, forgotten times. Then, with a royal gesture of disdain, they cast aside the lyre and reach for the trumpet, they speak in the spirit to the people and to coming nations. All their concentration, all their form, which is alive in them with mighty painfulness and often is much stronger and vaster than body and soul can bear, the innumerable, colorful figures, the activity and urgency of rhythm and harmony: all that—hear it, you artists! —is smothered people, is living people that have collected in them, that are buried in them and will be resurrected out of them.

And along with them there arise other individuals, whom a mixture of spirit and unspirit has isolated: tyrants, accumulators of wealth, leasers of men, robbers of land. In such beginnings of the time of decline and transition, as represented most pompously and magnificently in the Renaissance, or early Baroque period, these men still have many features of spirit, centrifugally dispersed but also partly concentrated in them. In all their mighty power they still have a trace of melancholy, rigidity, strangeness, and unearthly visionariness. In many of these phenomena one would almost say that something spiritlike, or rather, spectrelike, lives on, mightier than they, a content for which the container of isolated personality is too narrow. And very, very rarely one of them awakens as if out of a bad dream, flings away his crown and climbs on the top of Mount Horeb, to hold vigil for this people.

And sometimes mixed natures come, at whose cradle a fairy long hovered; it may make of them a great conqueror or a great freedom fighter, a genius of thought and of free fantasy or a great merchant: men like Napoleon and Ferdinand Lassalle.

And these isolated few, into whom richness of spirit and power has fled, face the many isolated, atomized people who are left only with unspirit, desolation and misery: the masses, who are called the people, but who are only a heap of uprooted, betrayed men. Uprooted, in melancholy strangeness, are the individuals, the few in whom the folk-spirit is buried, even if they know nothing of it. Uprooted, divided in hardship and destitution, are the masses into whom the spirit must again flow, if spirit and the people are to be reunited and revitalized.

Death is the atmosphere between us, for where there is no spirit, there is death. Death has crawled over our skin and penetrated into our flesh. But in us, in our hidden self, in our most secret and deepest dream and desire, in the figures of art, our strongest will, deep contemplative insight, purposeful action, love, despair and courage, psychic distress and joy, in revolution and unity, there life, power and glory dwell; spirit is hidden and generated and wishes to erupt and create a people with beauty and communality.

The times of the human race that shine most splendidly in subsequent history are those where this tendency of the seepage of the spirit out of the people into the ravines and hollows of solitary individuals has just begun and not yet progressed very far: where the common spirit, the society of societies, the interlinkage of the many associations springing from the spirit stand in full bloom, but where the persons of genius have already arisen, although still naturally controlled by the great spirit of the people, which therefore is not banally awed by their great works but rather accepts them as a natural fruit of communal life and rejoices in them with holy feelings. Thus it often hardly hands down the names of their originators to posterity.

The Golden Age of the Greek people was such a time; the Christian Middle Ages were such a time.

It was not an ideal; it was reality. And so we see along with the lofty, spontaneous spirituality, relics of former coercion and already the beginings of future coercion by external brutality, imposed force, the state. But the spirit was stronger; indeed often it permeated and embellished even such institutions of power and dependence, which become detestable instruments of cruelty in times of decay. Not everything historians call "slavery" was always completely such.

It was not an ideal, because spirit was there. Spirit gives meaning and sacredness to life; spirit makes, creates and permeates the present with joy, strength and delight. The ideal turns away from the present toward something new. It is a longing for the future, for something better and unknown. It is the road out of times of decline to a new culture.

Here one more point must be made. These times of glorious height which have reached their turning point were preceded by other periods, not only one single time in so-called development, but again and again in the rise and fall of successive and intermingling peoples. Binding spirit was there too, and a common life on a voluntary basis, by the natural compulsion of belonging together. But no cathedral spires, glittering with beauty in all details and coherent in specific harmony, towered heavenward, and no colonnaded halls stood in calm serenity against the transparent blueness of the sky. Those were simpler groups; no personalities of individual genius and subjectivity yet existed as the representatives of the people; it was a primitive, a communist life. There were — and there are — long centuries and often millennia of relative stagnation. Stagnation, hear it, you scholarly and liberal contemporaries, is for those times, for those peoples, which existed almost yesterday, a sign of their culture. Progress, what you call progress, this incessant hustle-bustle, this rapid tiring and neurasthenic, short-breathed chase after novelty, after anything new as long as it is new, this progress and the crazy ideas of the practitioners of development associated with it and the maniacal habit of saying good-bye immediately on arrival, this progress, this unsteady, restless haste, this inability to remain still and this perpetual desire to be on the move, this so-called progress is a symptom of our abnormal conditions, our unculture. We need something quite different from the symptoms of our depravity, in order to escape from it — there were and are, I say, times and peoples of prosperous life, times of tradition, epic times, of agriculture and rural craftsmanship, without much outstanding art, without much written science. Times that are less splendid and raise fewer monuments and gravestones to themselves than those great periods that are so glorious because their heirs are already with them and spend their still wonderful youth with them: a time rather of long and broad life, that almost could be called comfortable. The self-conscious spirit with its magic, coercive power did not yet exist. It was not yet in process of separating and spreading like a gospel throughout the world, subjecting the souls of men to its spell. There were such times too; and there are such peoples; and such times will return.

In such times the spirit seems hidden. Even with careful scrutiny one recognizes it almost only by its expression in the forms of social life and the economic institutions of the community.

Men have always returned to the very first, primitive beginnings, the first stages of these times when they had saved themselves from yet earlier times of decline, spiritlessness, tyranny, exploitation, and governmental power, often with the help of nations that, in this state of fertile stillness, moved slowly across the earth to new places and entered them, youthful and healthy, from out of unknown distance and obscurity. Thus the Romans and the Greeks of the late Imperial period were plunged into this rejuvenating bath and again became primitive children, ripe for the new spirit which came over them simultaneously from the East. There is, for the empathetic observer of mankind, in its eternal decline and eternal re-becoming, hardly anything more touching, more tormenting and at the same time arousing almost childishly pious confidence, as the works of early Byzantine art, which could equally be called late Greek. Through what depravity and through what tremendous re-establishment, through what horrors and what psychic distress generations passed in the transition from the stylish, elegant formalism and deadly coldness of virtuosity to this almost dreadfully sincere feeling, to this childish simplicity and inability to perceive corporeal reality correctly! The virtuosity of eye and hand would have been passed on from generation to generation in art and craft, if the soul had not spat it out as filth and bitter gall. What hopes, what deep consolations lie in so painful, yet refreshing a sight, for us and for all who can learn from it because they know: no progress, no technology, no virtuosity will bring us salvation and blessing. Only out of the spirit, only out of the depth of our inner need and inner richness will the great transformation which we call socialism come about.

But for us there is nothing so remote and unknown, no sudden surprise out of the darkness anywhere in the world. No analogy of the past can apply perfectly to us. The surface of the earth is known to us, we have our hand on it and our gaze sweeps around it. Peoples that were still separated from us by decades or millennia — the Japanese, the Chinese — are eagerly exchanging their static way of life for our progress, and their culture for our civilization. Other, smaller peoples of this state have been exterminated or depraved with our Christianity and alcohol. This time renewal must come from ourselves, although perhaps peoples of a new mixture, like the Americans, peoples of an older stage, like the Russians, the Indians, perhaps also the Chinese will help us most fruitfully in doing so.

The peoples who first climbed out of some state of depravity and escaped to the fabulous, epic times of a renewed intitial culture, of communism, were often for a long time not attracted by a new spirit in visible, tangible, expressive form. They did not have the splendor of an overpowering illusion holding them under its spell. But they had abandoned superstition, the pitiful, unrecognizable relic of former great periods. They sought only earthly happiness, and so their life began anew with the spirit of justice that permeated their institutions, their social life, their works and the distribution of goods. The spirit of justice as an earthly activity and creation of voluntary association, prior to a heavenly illusion that later would transfigure earthly activity into community and makes it, all the more, naturally cogent.

Am I, with these words, speaking of the barbarians of long past millenia? Am I speaking of the ancestors of the Arabs, Iroquois,

Greenlanders?

I don't know. We know so little of the changes and origins of these so-called barbaric peoples of former and present times. We have hardly any traditions and real evidence. We know only that the so-called primitive states of alleged barbarians or savages are not original in the sense of mankind beginning so, as many experts believe, who are educated beyond their mental capacity. We know of no such beginning. Even the cultures of the "barbarians" come from somewhere, have deep roots in humanity. Perhaps they descended from a barbarity like the one we are trying to escape.

For I am speaking of our own peoples; I am speaking of ourselves.

We are the people of the decline, whose pioneers have grown weary in the race for stupid power, for the shameful isolation and surrender of the individual. We are people of the descent where there is no longer a binding spirit but only the distorted relics, the nonsense of superstition, and its crude surrogate, the coercion of external power, the state. We are the people of the downfall and, therefore, of that type of downfall whose vanguard see no meaning that points beyond this earthly life, who can envisage no illusory heaven they could believe in and proclaim as sacred. We are the people that can stride upwards again only through one single spirit: the spirit of justice in the earthly matters of communal life. We are the people that can be saved and brought to culture only through socialism.

So our time stands between two ages. What does it look like?

A cohesive spirit — yes! yes! the word spirit does occur often in this book. Perhaps it happens because the men of our time, especially the so-called socialists, say "spirit" so seldom and act correspondingly. They do not act spiritually and so they do nothing real and practical; and how could they do anything real if they think so little! There is no cohesive spirit that impels men to spontaneously collaborate in matters of common interest, in the production and distribution of consumer goods. There is no spirit hovering above all work above every indus-trious impulse like the song of the lark out of the skies or the far-away song of invisible choruses, the spirit of art transfiguring earthly activity. There is no spirit that would impart necessity and freedom to natural drives, satisfactions, festivities. There is no spirit linking all life with eternity, sanctifying our senses, making all bodily functions heavenly, every activity a joy, a cause for exuberance and exhilaration.

What is there? God, who created the world; whose son redeems this world from sin... enough of that, of these misunderstood remnants of a symbolism that once made sense, remnants that are now taken literally and held up for belief down to the last dot and letter and miraculous tale, so that the so-called soul or even the body too can attain bliss after rotting in the grave. Enough of this. This spirit is an unspirit, has nothing to do with either truth or life. If anything is probably false, then it is these ideas as a whole.

And our scholars know it. If the people, a very large part of the people, are caught in the spirit of wrong and ruinous falsehood, then how many of our scholars are entangled in the spirit of deceit and cowardice.

And how many again, among the people and scholars, no longer are concerned with any spirit and think that there is nothing more superfluous than to bother with such things.

In school, children are educated in false teachings and their parents are forced to let their children's thinking be distorted. A horrible gap is opened between the children of the poor, who are kept in the old religion by force, and children of the rich, who are provided with all sorts of semi-enlightenment and mild doubt. The children of the poor are supposed to stay stupid, docile, timid, while the children of the rich become semi-educated and frivolous.

How is work done in our time? Why is work done?

What is—work?

Only a few animal species know what we call work: bees, ants, termites and men. The fox in his lair and on the hunt, the bird in its nest and catching insects or seeking grains—they all must strive, in order to live, but they do not work. Work is technique; technique is a common spirit and forethought. There is no work without spirit, forethought and communality.

What does the spirit governing our work look like? What is our forethought like? What is the nature of the communality that regulates our work?

It looks and is as follows:

A few men own the earth, and consequently the possibility of habitation, industry, and activity; the earth, and consequently the raw materials; the earth, and consequently the means of labor inherited from the past. These few men seek economic and personal power in the form of land ownership, monetary wealth, and domination over men.

They cause things to be produced, which they believe, according to the respective situation, the market will accept with the help of a great army of agents and sales representatives, or, in plain language, persuasive chatterers, wholesalers, retailers, newspaper advertisements and posters, fireworks and attractive packaging.

But even when they know that the market can absorb their commodities only with difficulty or not at all, or at least not at the desired price, they must continue to bombard it with their products: for their production plants and enterprises are not guided by the needs of a coherent organic class of men of a community or a larger association of consumers or of a people, but by the demands of their production machinery, to which thousands of workers are harnessed like Ixion on the wheel, because they can do nothing except perform small partial labors at these machines.

Whether they make cannons to exterminate men, or stockings out of spun dust or mustard out of ground peas, is irrelevant. Whether their commodities are used, whether they are useful or senseless, beautiful or ugly, fine or crude, of good quality or poor, is irrelevant. As long as they are bought, and bring in money.

The great mass of men is separated from the earth and its products, from the earth and the means of labor. They live in poverty and insecurity. There is no joy and meaning in their life. They work at things that have no connection with their life. They work in a way that makes them dull and joyless. Many, entire masses of men, often have no roof over their head. They freeze, starve, and die miserably.

Because they are undernourished and have inadequate housing, they catch tuberculosis or other diseases and die before their time. And those whose health survives the effects of poor housing and hardship, air pollution and disease-infected houses, are often destroyed by over-exertion, acrid dust, poisonous substances and vapors in the factory.

Their life has no links to nature, or only diminished ones. They do not know what pathos, joy, seriousness, interiority, what ecstasy and tragedy are. They do not experience themselves. They cannot smile or be childlike. They endure themselves and do not know how unbearable they are, for even mentally they live in dirt and polluted air, in a dense smoke of ugly words and repulsive pleasures.

The place where they congregate and foster their type of communality is not the free marketplace under the open sky and not a high cupola symbolizing closed coherence under the freedom and infinity of the sky, and no community hall and no guild hall and no bathhouse: their common meeting place is the tavern.

There they succumb to drink and can often no longer live without being intoxicated. They get drunk because nothing is so essentially alien to them as sobriety.

It is necessary to the system and predetermined that very many want to work and cannot, while many who could work no longer muster the will to do so; that many seeds are killed in the womb and very many children are killed after birth; that very many spend long years of life in prison or workhouse.

Prisons, jails, and gallows have had to be built. Property and life, health, a sound body and sexual freedom of choice are always threatened by the violence of miserable and depraved men. Rebels and violent felons are now generally not a threat and robbers are now less bold than formerly. Instead there are countless thieves, burglars and swindlers, and contracted killers called murderers.

Priests and middle class citizens who submit to moral restraint have introduced the practice of speaking of these poor wretches as if they were animals, though they are innocently guilty for our despicable innocence. They are called beasts, swine, goats and animals. You men, however, behold how they are like children: look at them and stare at their features, when they lie in the morgue. You have spared yourself too long and you have too long thought only of good clothes, your own flesh, and your notoriously sensitive hearts! Look at the poor. the miserable, the sunken, the criminals and whores, you good citizens, you withdrawn and reserved youths, you chaste girls and honorable women. Look and learn: your innocence is your guilt; your guilt is your life.

Their guilt is the life of prosperous men, except that they too have long since no longer been innocent and pleasant to contemplate. Hardship and unspirit create screaming ugliness, deprivation and desolation. Prosperity and unspirit beget desolation, emptiness and deceit.

And there is a point, a place where the two meet: the poor and the pitifully rich. The two meet in sexual distress. The very poorest are the young women who have nothing to sell but their bodies. The most pitiful are the young men who roam the streets and don't know where their sexuality comes from and what they are to do with it. No market and no cathedral dome, no temple and community house is now the communal place for all. Only where power and money dwell, where spirit would like to be at home, has pleasure so totally disappeared that there are people who seek to sell it and others who must buy their disgusting surrogate. When pleasure becomes a commodity, there is no longer any difference between the souls of the uppermost and of the lowermost; and the house of prostitution is the house of representatives of our time.

And the state exists to create order and the possibility to continue living amid all this spiritless nonsense, confusion, hardship and degeneracy. The state, with its schools, churches, courts, prisons, work-houses, the state with its army and its police; the state with its soldiers, officials and prostitutes.

Where there is no spirit and no inner compulsion, there is external force, regimentation, the state.

Where spirit is, there is society. Where unspirit is, there is the state. The state is the surrogate for spirit.

It is this in another sense as well.

Something that looks and acts like spirit must exist. Living men cannot for even a moment live without spirit. Materialists may be quite decent and proper, but they have no idea of what constitutes the world and life. What sort of spirit is it that permits us to stay alive? The spirit regulating our work is, on the one hand, money, and on the other, hardship as we have seen. The spirit that raises us above body and individuality among the lower classes is superstition, whore-mongering and alcohol; among the upper classes it is alcohol, whore-mongering and luxury. And so there are all sorts of spirits—away with them! Away with them! And the spirit that elevates the individuals into a totality, into a people, is called today the nation. Nation as natural coercion of the biological community is a primevally beautiful and ineradicable spirit. Nation in amalgamation with the state and with outrageous violence is an artificial crudity and malignant stupidity— and yet it is an *ersatz* for spirit, a psychic equivalent to the intoxicating alcoholic spirits that have become the habitual poison of men living today.

The state with its boundaries and the nations with their conflicts are substitutes for a non-existent spirit of the people and of community. The idea of the state is an artificial imitation of spirit, a false illusion, it couples purposes that have nothing to do with one another, that have no roots in the soil such as the beautiful interests of a common language and customs, the interests of economic life (and we have seen what economic life is today!) with a certain territory. The state, with its police and all its borders and institutions governing private property, exists for men's sakes as a miserable substitute for spirit and purposeful groups. Moreover the next step is to treat men as if they existed for the state which pretends to be a sort of ideal structure and self-purpose, i.e., once again, spirit. Spirit is something that dwells equally in the hearts and animated bodies of all individuals, which erupts out of them with natural compulsion as a binding quality and leads them to associate together. The state is never established inside the individual. It has never become an individual quality, never been voluntary. It resides rather in the centralism of command and discipline instead of in the center that rules the world of spirit: that is the heartbeat and free, independent thinking in the living body of the person. Once long ago there were communities, tribal groups, guilds, brotherhoods, corporations, societies, and they were all stratified into a society. Today there is force, the letter of the law, and the state.

And the state—which moreover is nothing, and in order to conceal this nothingness, is clad deceitfully in the mantle of nationality and deceitfully connects this nationality, which is a delicate spiritual bond between men, with a community occupying one geographical territory which has nothing to do with it and does not exist—this state thus seeks to be a spirit and ideal, an incomprehensible transcendental, as it were, for which millions slaughter one another with bloodthirsty enthusiasm. That is the extreme, the epitome of unspirit that has been introduced because the true spirit of unity has perished and ceased to exist. Yet let it be said: if men did not have this horrid superstition instead of the living truth of natural spiritual unity, they would be unable to live, for they would suffocate in the shame and degradation of this unlife and this disunity; they would crumble to dust like dry filth.

That is what our time looks like. There it stands between the ages. Do you who hear my words with your ears as whole men, do you feel that I could hardly proclaim this description? Do you feel I was compelled to speak of this terrible thing for your sake and that I called to your attention that which I no longer need discover myself, since this entire damnable environment has long since been a part of my basis in life, even of my physical stance and facial expression? Do you feel that I was bent under too ponderous a burden, that I was short-breathed and my heart pounded in my chest?

You people, one and all, who suffer under this outrage: let not only my voice reach you and the tone of my words. Hear also my silence and atonality, my choking anxiety. And see my clenched fist, my twisted features and the pale decisiveness of all my bearing. Grasp, above all, the inadequacy of this description and my inexpressible incapacity, *for I want people to hear me, stand by me, walk with me, people who, like me, can no longer bear it.*

4.

Socialism is the tendency of will of unified men to create something new for the sake of an ideal.

We have now seen why this new entity should be created. We have seen the old. Once again we have let the existing system pass before our shuddering eyes. Now I will not say, as some may well expect, how the new reality we desire should be constituted as a whole. I offer no depiction of an ideal, no description of a utopia. I have given some idea of what can now be said and I have called it by name: justice. An image has been delineated of our conditions, and of our people; does anyone believe that reason and decency, or even love, need only be preached in order to happen?

Socialism is a cultural movement, a struggle for beauty, greatness, abundance of the peoples. No one can understand it, no one can lead to it, unless he sees that socialism comes down from the centuries and millennia. Whoever does not grasp socialism as a step ahead in a long, hard history, knows nothing of it; and this already means — we will hear yet more of it — that no everyday politicians can be socialists. The socialist grasps the whole of society and of the past; feels and knows whence we come and then determines where we are headed.

That mark distinguishes the socialist from the politician. He is interested in the whole, and he grasps our conditions in their totality, in their historical context; he thinks holistically. It then follows that he rejects the entirety of our forms of life, that he has no other intent and goal but the whole, the universal, the principle.

Not only what he rejects, not only what he aims to achieve is comprehensive and universal for the socialist. His means, too, cannot cling to the particular; the roads he travels on are not side roads, but main roads.

Whether great love predominates in him, or imagination, or clear observation, or nausea, or a wild aggressiveness, or strong rational thought, or whatever else may be his motivation; whether he is a thinker or a poet, a fighter or a prophet: the true socialist will always have a vital element of the universal in him. However he will never be (I am speaking here of mentality, not of external professions) a professor, an advocate, an accountant, a stickler for detail, a bragging dilettante, a typical person.

Here is the place to say what must be said (because it has just been said): those who call themselves socialists today are, one and all, not socialists. What now goes by the name of socialism is absolutely not socialism. Here too, in this so-called socialist movement, as in all organizations and institutions of these times, a pitiful, crude surrogate has replaced spirit. But here the counterfeit substitute is especially bad, especially obvious and ridiculous to anyone who has seen through it, but particularly dangerous for those it deceives. This surrogate is a caricature, an imitation, a travesty of the spirit. Spirit is a grasping of the whole in a living universal. Spirit is a unity of separate things, concepts and men. In times of transition, spirit is ardent enthusiasm, courage in the struggle. Spirit is constructive activity. What today simulates socialism also seeks to grasp a whole and also wishes to place details under general categories. But since no living spirit dwells in it, since what it looks at does not come to life, and since its universal does not become creative, since it has no intuitive impulse, its universal does not become true knowledge and true will. Spirit has been replaced by an eccentric and ludicrous scientific superstition. No wonder that this weird doctrine is a travesty of spirit, since its origin weas already a travesty of real spirit, namely Hegelian philosophy. The man who concocted this drug in his laboratory was called Karl Marx. Professor Karl Marx. He brought us scientific superstition instead of spiritual knowledge, politics and party instead of cultural will. But since, as we will see below, his science contradicts his politics and every party reality, and moreover from day to day more obviously contradicts reality; since a so thoroughly false imitation of the universal as this science can never, in the long run, maintain itself against the tangible day-to-day realities of individual phenomena, the revolt of the spiritless party activists, detail-mongers and bragging dilettantes has been played off against the travesty of science. It will be shown here, however, that there is something else, and that neither the former nor the latter are socialists. Here it will be said that neither Marxism nor the patchwork of the revisionists is socialism. Here it will be shown what socialism is not, and what it is. Let us see.

Marxism

Karl Marx artificially bridged the two components of Marxism, science and the political party, creating something apparently completely new, which the world had never seen before, namely scientific politics and the party with a scientific basis and a scientific program. That really was something new and, moreover, modern and timely, and furthermore it flattered the workers to hear that precisely they represented science, indeed the very latest science. If you want to win the masses, then flatter them. If you want to incapacitate them for serious thought and action and make their representatives archetypes of hollow infatuation, mouthing a rhetoric which they themselves at best only half understand, then convince them that they represent a scientific party. If you want to fill them completely with malicious stupidity, then train them in party schools. The scientific party, thus, was the demand of the most advanced men of all times! What amateurs all previous politicians had been, who acted from instinct or geniality as one walks, thinks, writes or paints. Though this does require, along with natural talent, a great deal of skill and technique, it is by no means a science. And what modest people those representatives of politics as a sort of science had been, from Plato through Machiavelli down to the author of the excellent *Handbook for the Demagogue*. With great skill and a strong eye for simplification and synthesis, they arranged and classified individual experiences and institutions, but the idea never occurred to them to do this scientifically. What aesthetics would be if it purported to provide the programmatic basis for artistic creativity, Marxism is for these scientific socialists.

In reality, however, the scientific delusion of Marxism accords badly with the practical politics of the party. They go well together only for such men as Marx and Engels, or Kautsky, who combine the professor and the wire-puller in one person. Certainly one can want what is right and worthwhile only if one knows what one wants, but — apart from the fact that such knowledge is far from a so-called science — it is almost a contradiction to claim, on the one hand, on the basis of so-called historical laws of development which have the supposed force of natural laws, exact knowledge of how things must necessarily and inevitably come, so that neither the will or action of any man could change this predetermination in the slightest, while on the other hand, to be a political party which can do nothing else but will, demand, influence, act, and change particulars. The bridge between these two incompatibilities is the maddest arrogance ever exposed to public view in the history of man. Everything the Marxists do or demand (for they demand more than they do) is precisely at the moment a necessary link of development, determined by Providence, and only the manifestation of natural law. Everything others do is a futile attempt to hold back the inexorable historical tendencies discovered and secured by Karl Marx. In other words the Marxists, in their goals, are the executive organs of the law of development. They are the discoverers and also the implementers of this law, more or less like the legislative and executive branches of the government of nature and society combined in one person. The others, in any case, also help to implement these laws, but against their will. The poor fellows always want the wrong thing but all their effort and activity only help the necessity determined by the science of Marxism. Every arrogance, every obstinate craze, intolerance and narrow-minded injustice, and the whole sardonic temper constantly displayed by the scientifico-political heart of the Marxists stems from their absurd and peculiar amalgamation of theory and practice of science and party. Marxism is the professor who wants to rule; it is thus the legitimate offspring of Karl Marx. Marxism is a concoction that resembles its father; and the Marxists resemble their doctrine, except that the intellectual acuity, the thorough knowledge and the often laudable gift of logical combination and association of the real Professor Marx is now often replaced by pamphleteer scholarship, party-school wisdom, and plebeian parroting. Karl Marx at least studied the facts of economic life, the documentary source-material and — often even quite unabashedly — the revelations of great intuitive geniuses; his successors are often satisfied with compendia and textbooks compiled with the approval of the Ministry of Education in Berlin. And since we here do not have to go along with the foolish and shameless flattery of the proletariat, since socialism aims at the abolition of the proletariat and therefore need not find it to be an institution especially beneficial to the mind and heart of all concerned (for great and fortunate personalities, it will, of course, like every hardship and impediment, bring with it a good many advantages; and there is always hope that privation and inner emptiness, insofar as they constitute a sort of readiness or open possibility of fulfillment, and tension, will someday, at the great moment, suddenly impel entire masses to act in solidarity and genius), it can thus be said here once more: it is true, a miracle can one day come over the proletariat, as over any other people, namely the miracle of the spirit, but Marxism was no such Pentecostal miracle and it brought no gift of tongues, rather only Babylonian confusion and flatulence. The proletarian professor, the proletarian lawyer and party leader is that caricature of caricatures called Marxism, the kind of socialism that claims to be a science.

What does this science of Marxism teach? What does it claim? It claims to know the future. It presumes to have such deep insight into eternal laws of development and the determinant factors of human history that it knows what is to come, how history will continue and what will become of our conditions and forms of production and organization.

Never has the value and meaning of science been so ridiculously misunderstood. Never has mankind, especially the most oppressed, intellectually deprived and underdeveloped part of mankind, been so mocked with a distorted mirror-image.

Here we are not yet even considering the content of this science, of the supposed course of mankind the Marxists claim to have discovered. At this point it is only a matter of revealing, mocking and rejecting the immeasurably foolish presumption that a science exists that can reveal, calculate and determine the future with certainty from the data and news of the past and the facts and conditions of the present.

To this point I have also tried to speak of where we have come from, as I believe — I could venture to say, as I *know* for I am not afraid of being misunderstood by dolts, in fact I hope to be — and where, in my deepest conviction and feeling, we are going, must go, and must want to go. But this necessity is not imposed upon us in the form of a natural law, but of *what ought to be.* For if I say that I know something, is it in the sense that in mathematics an unknown quantity is calculated from known ones? Or that a geometrical problem can be solved? Or that the law of gravity and inertia or the law of the conservation of energy are always valid? Or that I can calculate the trajectory of a falling object or projectile if I know the data required for the formula? Or that I know that H_2O is water? Or that we can calculate the movements of many stars and predict eclipses of the moon and sun? No! All these are scientific activities and results. They are natural laws because they are laws of our mind. But there is also a natural law, a law of our mind, a sub-law of the great law of the conservation of energy, that says: what we will make of our life and body, what the continuation of our previous life, the road ahead, the release of compression, the activation of disposition will be — all this is called "the future" — cannot be presented in the form of science, i.e., of accomplished facts subject to classification, but only in the form of a feeling accompanying a disposition, of the inner pressure of effort and desire exactly adequate of the external, shifting state of balance. This implies will, duty, intimation all the way to prophecy, vision and artistic creation. The point of the road where we are standing is not analogous to a mathematical problem or a factual report or even a law of development; that would be a mockery of the law of the conservation of energy. This road corresponds to a dare-devil audacity. Knowledge means: to have lived, to possess what has been. Life means: to live, creating and suffering what is to come.

Not only does it mean that there is no science of the future; it also implies that there is only a living knowledge of the still living past, but no inert science as of something dead and lying there. The Marxists and, like them, all moralists and politicians of development, whether they adhere to the theory of catastrophic and diametrical development like the pre-Darwinian Marxists or wish to posit an evenly advancing progress by means of a slow, gradual accumulation of minute changes, like the Darwinistic revisionists, these and all representatives of the science of development should, if they are absolutely unable to give up scientific activity, conduct a scientific investigation of what the following, splendid, releated group of words have as their real meaning, what they express of the truth of nature and spirit, namely these words: *I know, I can, I may, I will, it must, and I should*. This would make them more modest and scientific, more human and congenial, and more enterprising and manly.

Thus history and political economics are not sciences. The forces at work in history cannot be scientifically formulated; their judgement will always be an estimate describable by a higher or lower name, depending on the human nature it contains or radiates — prophecy or professorial nonsense. It will always be a valuation dependent on our nature, our character, our life and our interests. Furthermore, even if the forces in question were as surely known to us as they are formless, faltering, indeterminate and changing, the facts necessary for the application of such principles are very poorly known. What external facts for scientific treatment do we have after all for the literally infinite past of man and the world? Of course, all sorts of things, far too many, have been transported and unloaded in the carts of this so-called science. Unfortunately they are confused, desolate and fragmentary debris, dumped helter-skelter, from one second of the so-called history of men and the world. No example is crude enough to clarify how little we know. Of course, one case is, as the splendid Goethe says, often worth a thousand words and contains them, for the intuitive genius. However, for this entire area of biological becoming and human history there are exemplary cases of forces and laws, but, again to use Goethe's language, these become simply the experiential manure of the data-collectors, Darwinists and revisionists, and the dialectical manure of the Marxists. And so the genius, for whom in matters of human coexistence one case is often worth a thousand words, is not a genius of science but a genius of creation and action. Knowledge of life is involved, but it is not a science, however much it may be based on genuine, great science.

And, thank god and the world that it is so! For why live, if we knew, really knew, everything that is to come? Doesn't to live mean: to become new? Doesn't to live mean: as the old, secure, self-confident and independent being that we are, as a self-contained world and eternal entity, to enter into the new, uncertain other world that we are not, equally eternal, from gate to gate and multitude to multitude?

For when we call ourselves alive, are we readers or observers or beings driven by well-known forces into an equally well-known terrain, from the old to the old? Or are we not the striding foot and the working hand rather than the objects of action? And does not the world seem to us, every morning when we get up, vague, unknown and amorphous, like something new and presented, which we form and assimilate with the instrument of our own natural capacities? O you Marxists, if only you had abundance and fullness of joy in your private life, then you would not want to and you could not turn life into a science! And how could you, if you knew that your task as socialists is to help men attain forms and communities of joyous work and joyous living communality.

Not resigned, skeptical, or plaintive, but assenting joyously, I state that we know nothing of the manifold and incomprehensible forms of the past and future life of men and nations; I am proud and courageous enough to know, feel and live internally, more than many others, the destiny of the millennia. I do have an idea of what has happened and of what is underway. I do have a feeling as to the course of our destiny. I know where I want to go and where to advise and lead others, and I do wish to transmit my insight, my ardent feeling, my strong will to many, both individuals and masses. But am I speaking in formulae? Am I a journalist masquerading deceptively as a mathematician? Am I a Pied Piper of Hamlin leading immature children with the flute of science into the mountain of nonsense and fraud? Am I a Marxist?

No, but I will say what I am. I need not wait until the others of whom I am speaking, the Marxists, tell me. I have studied, researched and accumulated knowledge as well as anybody, and if there were a science of history and economics, then I surely would have brains enough to have learned it. For really, you are strange people, you Marxists, and it is surprising that you do not wonder about yourselves. Is it not an old and certain matter that even people of modest intelligence can learn the results of science once these results are there? What, then, is the point of all your quarreling, polemics and agitation, all your demands and negotiations, all your rhetoric and argumentation: if you have a science, cease these superfluous bickerings, take up the schoolmaster's cane and instruct us, teach us, let us learn and zealously practice the methods, operations, constructions, and as experienced, undeceived, and certain knowers, do what your Bebel has tried as an honest amateur: tell us at last the exact data of future history!

So I too have studied, not like you, but better than you and yet I say: what I teach is certainly not a science. Let each one examine whether his nature, his real life leads him on this same way, and let him come along with me only then, but let him come. I have studied better than you because I have something you don't have. Of course, my arrogance, or what is commonly so called, is not greater than yours. I would keep to myself my modest, i.e., appropriate, opinion of myself, as a matter-of-course among peers, except for the compulsion to say who is a socialist and who is not. For the cold-minded men of Niselheim, who have usurped socialism, and who watch over Marx's *Capital* like the dwarves guarding the Nibelungen treasure must be despised and dispersed. Socialism must be conveyed to its rightful heirs, so that it can become what it is: a joy and a jubilation, a building and making, a dream dreamed to its conclusion that now is to become a fulfillment in action and for all senses and all primary life. And because the heirs are still sleeping and sojourning in the faraway lands of dream and formalism and because someone must at last put a hand to the heritage, I must gather the heirs and legitimate myself as one of them.

Where, then, do the Marxists get all their scientific superstition? They want to reduce the variegated, fragmented, complicated and confused details of tradition and of the conditions to one line of order and unity. They too feel the need for simplification, unity, and universality.

Have we again reached you, O splendid redemptive One and Universal Idea, you that are as necessary to true thought as to true life, that create coexistence and community, agreement and interiority, and that are the idea in the mind of thinkers and the covenant of nature? you that are called by name: spirit!

But they do not have you, and therefore they replace you. Therefore they concoct their illusory counterfeit, the surrogate product of their historical patchwork and their scientific laws: they recognize only one convincing general principle that forms, correlates and coordinates details and connects scattered facts, namely: science. Indeed science is spirit, order, unity and solidarity: when it is science. But when it is a swindle and monkey-business, when the supposed man of science is only a journalist in disguise and badly camouflaged editorial writer, when statistically formulated heaps of facts and dialectically masked platitudes claim to be a sort of higher mathematics of history and an infallible instruction-manual for future life; then this so-called science is unspirit, an impediment to the intellect. It is an obstacle that must be eliminated with arguments and laughter, with blazing anger.

You do not know the other forms of the spirit and so you have put the professorial mask in front of your lawyer's faces, except when you are real professors who want to play prophet, as that other professor, your patron saint, wanted to play the lute, but could not.

But we know what spirit is and we have often said it here. We have a universal coherence in the course of mankind that is different in kind and origin from yours. Our knowledge is imbued with our great basic feelings and our strong, far-ranging will: we are—

but first, poor Marxists, take a chair and sit down and hold fast; for a terrible, presumptuous assertion is about to follow, which at the same time preempts an accusation that you would have liked to make against me in a contemptuous tone—

We are poets; and we want to eliminate the scientific swindlers, the Marxists, cold, hollow, spiritless, so that poetic vision, artistically concentrated creativity, enthusiasm, and prophecy will find their place to act, work and build from now on; in life, with human bodies, for the harmonious life, work and solidarity of groups, communities and nations.

Yes, indeed. What has now long enough been a poetic dream and melody, a fascinating contour and a brilliant array of colors, shall come to full actualization and become true. We poets want to create in the living medium and see who is the greater and stronger practitioner: you who claim to know, and do nothing or we, who now have in us the living image, the certain feeling, and the energetic will. It is we who wish to do whatever can be done, now and forever, relentlessly, who wish to organize people who are with us into a forward-moving wedge, on and on, in action, construction and demolition, incessantly, passing you by with laughter, reasons and anger, and overcoming denser clods with attacks and battles. We provide no science and no party. We provide still less an intellectual alliance, as you understand it, for when you speak of such a thing, you have in mind what you call enlightenment, and what we call semi-education and pamphlet-fodder. The spirit that impels us is a quintessence of life and it creates effective reality. This spirit is called by another name: solidarity [*Bund*]; and what we seek to poeticize in beautiful presentation is: practice, socialism, a league [*Bund*] of working people.

Here we now see clearly before our eyes and we can touch with our hands why the Marxists have excluded the spirit from their famous conception of history, which they call materialist. We can at this point present the explanation better than other excellent opponents of the Marxists have succeeded in doing. The Marxists have, in their declarations and views, excluded the spirit for a very natural, indeed almost excellent material reason: namely, because they have no spirit.

But if it were only true that their manner of describing history could rightly be called "materialistic." That would be a laudable, even gigantic enterprise, though one which their representatives could not achieve with a spirit of their own: the attempt to describe the whole of human history merely in the form of physical events, corporeally real processes, of an unending interaction between the material events of the rest of the world and the physiological processes of human bodies. It could, however, for the reasons I have already stated, by no means be a science based on laws, but could only become an imaginative, almost fantastic preliminary sketch of such a science. Perhaps someday someone will undertake it, even if it were only to find the right basis and the possibility of language, and to melt this rigid structure and reduce it completely to an image and to undertake the great reversal, i.e., to depict the whole of human history—excluding all corporeality—as a psychic total happening, as the exchange of mental currents. For whoever can think materialism through to its ultimate consequences knows that it is only the other side of idealism. Whoever is such a genuine materialist can come only from the school of Spinoza. But enough of that! What do the Marxists understand of that? The Marxists, who, when they hear the name Spinoza, probably think of the stuffed doll their pamphleteers and the Darwinistic monistic writers have made of Spinoza.

Enough of that: here it is necessary only to say that what the

Marxists call a materialist conception of history has nothing whatever
to do with any rationally conceived materialism: in the end they even
considered it a contradiction to conceive of materialism rationally,
and they would not even have been wrong. At any rate, the historical
conception they teach ought to be called "economic." Its true name is,
as said above, the spiritless conception of history.

For they claim to have discovered that all political conditions,
religions, intellectual movements whatsoever, not excluding of course
their own doctrine and their whole agitation and political activity, are
only the ideological superstructure, a sort of epiphenomenon of
the economic conditions and social institutions and processes.
Their superficial minds are only slightly bothered by how
much mental and spiritual activity is inextricably interwoven with
what they call economic and social reality, by the fact that economic
life is only a tiny part of social life and that this social life is totally
inseparable from the great and small spiritual structures and
movements of human coexistence. Typically in all their pronouncements they are fast talkers and chatterers who have never felt the need
to fathom their own words. Had they ever done so they would have
become deep silent men, for they would have suffocated in all their
contradictions and incoherences.

This contradictory misuse of words has bothered the Marxists but
only as shallow men can be annoyed. Some adjust to the contradiction
by one absurd half-truth, others through a different distorted
falsehood, and so different schools and all sorts of tensions and
divisions arose among them. From this doctrine some conclude that
Marxism proclaims an apolitical and almost anti-political attitude,
since it reduces politics to an almost irrelevant reflection of the
economy. Politics, legislation and forms of government do not matter
but only economic forms and economic struggles (but of course these
struggles too are only smuggled into the pure doctrine, for a struggle,
even an economic one, is a thoroughly spiritual matter, strongly
interwoven with the life of the spirit—enough of this, for, as said
above, whoever investigates any point of Marxism always discovers
impossibility, compromise and contraband). Others, nonetheless,
want to influence economic matters with the help of politics and they
add to the compromises, excuses and tiresome emendation of reality,

which looks quite different from their professorial ink-blots. They add to these palliatives which they all must make. That is not the point, and we will deal no further with these disputed questions. May the politico-Marxists fight them out with their brothers, the syndicalists and the anarcho-socialists, recently so-called by a pitiful misuse of two noble names.

For the entire doctrine is false and does not hold water, and all that remains true and valuable is a fact that was realized in England and elsewhere long before Karl Marx: in contemplating human events the eminent significance of economic and social conditions and changes should not be ignored. This point culminated in the great movement which must be called the discovery of society as distinct from the state, one of the earliest and most important steps toward freedom, culture, solidarity, the people, and socialism. Many beneficial and seminal ideas are contained in the great writings of the political economists and brilliant journalists of the eighteenth century and the first socialists of the nineteenth. Marxism, however, has reduced all this to a caricature, a counterfeit and a corruption. The so-called science which the Marxists have made of it is in its real effect a pitiful and disastrous attempt (for no alleged science is so stupid as not to attract educated and uneducated masses, and also university professors, if it has a demagogic or even only a popular stamp), so Marxism tries to reverse the current leading away from the state, i.e., away from unculture to voluntary associations united by a common spirit, the current that carries with it the society of societies, back to the state and to the unspirit of all our social institutions, and moreover it harnesses this current to turn the wheels of ambitious politicians.

We must look at this more closely. For we have peeled off only two layers of the acrid Marxist onion, we must cut deeper into its center even if it brings tears to our eyes. We must further dissect the monstrosity, and I promise: there will always be a little snorting and sneezing and some laughter, as we continue. We have already seen what the case is with the science and the materialism of the Marxists: but what kind of historical course of the past, present and future have they discovered? Certainly not the one that grew from material reality into their spiritual superstructure, probably in their Cartesian pineal gland.

We have now reached the point where the professor who reduces life to a false science, human bodies to paper, himself is now transformed into a professor of quite a different sort, with quite other talents for transformation. Professors, after all, usually call themselves transformation artists, magicians, prestidigitators, who produce their sleight-of-hand feats and voluble eloquence at county fairs. Karl Marx's most famous and decisive chapters have always reminded me of this type of professor. "One, two, three. Don't believe what you see."

Consequently, according to Karl Marx, the progressive career of our nations from the Middle Ages via the present to the future, is a course that takes place "with the necessity of a natural process" (according to the English text, which is still clearer: with the necessity of a natural law), moreover with increasing rapidity. In the first stage, of petty shopkeepers, only average men, mediocrities, petit-bourgeois and that sort of pitiful persons exist, and very many people still own each their own very small property. Then comes capitalism, the second stage, the up-swing to progress, the first stage of development and the road to socialism, and the world looks altogether different. A few have each very large properties, the mass has nothing. The transition to this stage was hard, and it could not be done without violence and ugly deeds. However at this stage progress toward the promised land goes more and more rapidly and easily on the well-oiled rails of development. Thank God, more and more masses are proletarianized; thank God, there are ever fewer capitalists, they expropriate one another until finally masses of proletarians, like sand at the seashore, face isolated gigantic entrepreneurs and now leap to the third stage. the second process of development, the last step to socialism is only child's play: "The death-knell of capitalist private property strikes." The "centralization of the means of production" and the "socialization of labor," says Karl Marx, were achieved under capitalism. He calls this a mode of production that "flourished under the monopoly of capital," as he always easily falls into poetic rapture when he eulogizes the last beauties of capitalism just before it turns into socialism. Now the time has come: "capitalist production, with the necessity of a natural process, generates its own negation:" socialism. For "cooperation" and "the common ownership of the earth," says Karl Marx, is already an "accomplishment of the capitalist era." The great, enormous, almost infinite masses of proletarized men, really can contribute almost nothing to socialism. They must simply wait for the time to come. Yet is it not true? Are we far from reaching the point, you gentlemen of science, when capitalism could be said to have brought us cooperation and the common ownership of the earth and the means of production? Whatever common ownership means, this much at least is clear, however many different forms of common ownership there can be, it must be something else than usurpation, privilege, private property. Can any trace be seen now of this common ownership that supposedly already resembles socialism? Yes or no? For we would very much like to know how much longer this natural process will take. Show us your science, please!

But who knows, who knows! Perhaps Karl Marx saw the traces or the visible beginnings of common ownership of the earth and the means of production developing out of monopolistic capitalism already in the middle of the nineteenth century. For as far as cooperation is concerned, the matter is, on closer examination, already quite unambiguous. For me, however, cooperation means action together and common work, and if one is not a fool who calls the common pulling of a cow and a horse before a plow, or the work of Negro slaves on a cotton plantation or sugar-cane field in a common place and with common division of labor "cooperation" or working together" — but what am I saying? Karl Marx is just like that fool! What future! What further development of capitalism! The intelligent scholar stuck to the present. What Karl Marx called cooperation that is supposed to be an element of socialism is — the form of work which he saw in the capitalist enterprise of his time, the factory system, where thousands work in one room, the adaptation of the worker to the machines and the resulting pervasive division of labor in the production of commodities for the capitalist world market. For he says unquestioningly that capitalism is "already actually based on the social production enterprise!"

Yes indeed, such unparalleled nonsense goes against the grain, but it is certainly Karl Marx's true opinion that capitalism develops socialism completely out of itself and that the socialist mode of production "flourishes" under capitalism. We already have cooperation, we already are at least well on the road to common ownership of the earth and the means of production. In the end nothing will be left to do but chase away the few remaining owners. Everything else has blossomed from capitalism. For capitalism is equated with progress, society and even socialism. The true enemy is "the middle classes, the small industrialist, the small merchant, the craftsman, the farmer." For they work, themselves, and have at most a few helpers and apprentices. That is the bungler, the dwarf-enterprise, while capitalism is uniformity, the work of thousands in one place, work for the world market; that is social production and socialism.

That is Karl Marx's true doctrine: when capitalism has gained complete victory over the remnants of the Middle Ages, progress is sealed and socialism is practically here.

It is not symbolically significant that the foundation of Marxism, the Bible of this sort of socialism is called *Capital?* We oppose this capitalist socialism with our own socialism, saying: socialism, culture and solidarity, just exchange and joyous work, the society of societies can come only when a spirit awakens such as the Christian and pre-Christian era of the Teutonic nations knew it, and when this spirit does away with the unculture, dissolution and decline, which in economic terms is called: capitalism.

Thus two opposite things stand in sharp contrast.

Here Marxism—there socialism!

Marxism—unspirit, the paper blossom on the beloved thornbush of capitalism.

Socialism—the new force against rottenness; the culture that rises against the combination of un-spirit, hardship, and violence, against the modern state and modern capitalism.

And now one could understand what I want to say to its face against this no less modern thing, Marxism: it is the plague of our time and the curse of the socialist movement. Now it will be said even more clearly that it is so, why it is so, and why socialism can come about only in mortal enmity toward Marxism.

For Marxism is, above all, the philistine who looks down upon and despises everything past, who calls whatever suits him the present or the beginning of the future, who believes in progress, who likes 1908 better than 1907, who expects something quite special from 1909, and almost a final eschatological miracle from something so far off as 1920.

Marxism is the philistine and therefore the friend of everything mass-like and comprehensive. Something like a medieval republic of cities or a village *mark* or a Russian *mir* or a Swiss *Allmend* or a communist colony cannot for him have the least similarity with socialism, but a broad, centralized state already resembles his state of the future quite closely. Show him a country at a period when the small peasants prosper, when highly skilled trades flourish, when there is little misery, he will contemptuously turn up his nose; Karl Marx and his successors thought they could make no worse accusation against the greatest of all socialists, Proudhon, than to call him a petit-bourgeois and petit-peasant socialist, which was neither incorrect nor insulting, since Proudhon showed splendidly to the people of his nation and his time, predominantly small farmers and craftsmen, how they could have achieved socialism immediately without waiting for the tidy progress of big capitalism. However, believers in progress do not at all want to hear us speak of a possibility that was once there and yet did not become reality, and the Marxists and those infected by them cannot stand to hear anyone speak of a socialism that could have been possible before the downward movement which they call the upward movement of sacred capitalism. We, on the other hand, do not separate a fabulous development and social processes from what men want, do, could have wanted, and could have done. We know, however, that the determination and necessity of all that happens, including, of course, will and action, is valid and without exception, but only after the fact, i.e., after a reality is already there, does it thus become a necessity. When something did not happen, it was thus not possible, because, for example, men to whom urgent appeals were addressed and to whom reason was preached with fervor did not want to and could not be reasonable. Aha! the Marxists will interject triumphantly, Karl Marx however predicted that there was no possibility for that. Yes sir, we answer, and thereby he assumed a certain part of the guilt that it did not come about. He was for then, and for a long time afterwards, one of the guilty hinderers. In our opinion, human history does not consist of anonymous processes and a mere accumulation of many small mass events and omissions. For us the bearers of history are persons, and for us there are also guilty persons. Does anyone believe that Proudhon did not, like every prophet, every herald, more strongly than any cold scientific observers, often in great hours sense the impossibility of leading these his people to what he considered the most beautiful and most natural possibility? Anyone who thinks that faith in fulfillment is part of the great deeds, visionary behavior and urgent creativity of the apostles and leaders of mankind, knows them badly. Faith in their sacred truth is certainly a part of it, but also despair in men and the feeling of impossibility! Where overwhelming change and renewal have occurred, it is the impossible and incredible that is precisely the usual factor that brought about change.

But Marxism is uncultured, and it therefore always points, full of mockery and triumph, at failures and futile attempts and has such a childish fear of defeat. It shows greater contempt for nothing else than what it calls experiments or failures. It is a shameful sign of disgraceful decline, especially for the German people, whom such fear of idealism, enthusiasm and heroism so poorly fits, that such pitiful characters are the leaders of its enslaved masses. But the Marxists are for the impoverished masses exactly what nationalists have been since 1870 for the satiated classes of people: worshippers of success. Thus we grasp another, more accurate meaning of the term "materialist conception of history." Yes indeed, the Marxists are materialists in the ordinary, crude, popular sense of the word, and just like the nationalistic blockheads, they strive to reduce and exterminate idealism. What the nationalistic bourgeois has made of the German students, the Marxists have made of broad segments of the proletariat, cowardly little men without youth, wildness, courage, without joy in attempting anything, without sectarianism, without heresy, without originality and individuality. But we need all that. We need attempts. We need the expedition of a thousand men to Sicily. We need these precious Garibaldi-natures, and we need failures upon failures and the tough nature that is frightened by nothing, that holds firm and endures and starts over and over again until it succeeds, until we are through, until we are unconquerable. Whoever does not take upon himself the danger of defeat, of loneliness, of set-backs, will never attain victory. O you Marxists, I know how bad that sounds in your ears, you who fear nothing except what you call stabs in the back. That word belongs to your special vocabulary and perhaps with some right, since you show the enemy your back more than your face. I know how deeply you hate and how repulsive and unpleasant your dry temperaments find such fiery natures as the constructive Proudhon and the destructive Bakunin or Garibaldi. Everything Latin or Celtic, everything that smacks of the open air and wildness and initiative is almost embarassing to you. You have plagued yourselves enough to exclude everything free, personal or youthful, which you call stupidities, from the party, the movement and the masses. Truly, things would be better for socialism and our people if instead of the systematic stupidity, which you call your science, we had the fiery-headed stupidities of hot-tempered men brimming over with enthusiasm, which you cannot stand. Yes indeed, we want to do what you call experiments. We want to make attempts. We want to create from the heart, and then we want, if it must be, to suffer shipwreck and bear defeat, until we have the victory and land is sighted. Ashen-faced, drowsy men, cynical and uncultured, are leading our people; where are the Columbus natures, who prefer to sail the high seas in a fragile ship into the unknown rather than wait for developments? Where are the young, joyous victorious Reds who will laugh at these gray faces? The Marxists don't like to hear such words, such attacks, which they call relapses, such enthusiastic unscientific challenges. I know, and that is exactly why I feel so good at having told them this. The arguments I use against them are sound and they hold water, but if instead of refuting them with arguments I annoyed them to death with mockery and laughter, that would also suit me fine.

Thus the uncultured Marxist is much too clever, level-headed and cautious ever to think that capitalism in a state of total collapse, as was the case during the February revolution in France, might be confronted with socialist organization, just as he prefers to kill the forms of living community from the Middle Ages that were saved particularly in Germany, France, Switzerland, Russia, during centuries of decline and to drown them in capitalism rather than to recognize that they contain the seeds and living crystals of the coming socialist culture. However if one shows him the economic conditions, say, of England from the middle of the nineteenth century, with its desolate factory system, with the depopulation of the countryside, the homogenization of the masses and of misery, with economies geared to the world market instead of to real needs, he finds social production, cooperation, the beginnings of common ownership. He feels at home.

The real Marxist, if he has not yet become uncertain and begun to make concessions (nowadays, of course, these endangered Marxists have been making all sorts of concessions for quite some time), wants nothing to do with farm cooperatives, credit unions, or worker cooperatives, even if they show magnificent development, while capitalist department stores make an altogether different impression on him, for so much organizational spirit is expended in them on unproductive robbery and usurpation, and on the sale of worthless trash.

But has any Marxist ever been concerned with this great, decisive question: *what* is produced for the world market, *what* is dumped on the consumers? Their gaze is always locked only on the external, inessential, superficial forms of capitalist production, which they call social production, which we must now discuss.

Marxism is the uncultured plodder who knows nothing more important, nothing more splendid, nothing more sacred than technology and its progress. Put such a plodder face to face with Jesus, who in his richness and the generosity of his inexhaustible personality, as well as in his significance for the spirit and for life, is also a tremendous socialist, put him before the living Jesus on the cross and before a new machine for the transportation of men or freight. If he is honest and not a cultural hypocrite, he will find the crucified Son of Man to be a totally useless and superfluous phenomenon and will go running after the machine.

And yet how much more this quiet, calmly suffering greatness of heart and spirit has truly moved than all the transport machines of these times!

And yet where would all the transport machines of our times be without this quiet, calmly suffering greatness on mankind's cross.

That too had to be said here, although only those who already knew it will readily understand what it means.

The boundless reverence of the adulators of progress for technology is the key to understanding the origin of Marxism. The father of Marxism is neither the study of history, nor Hegel. It is neither Smith nor Ricardo, nor one of the pre-Marxist socialists. It is neither a revolutionary democratic condition, nor even less the will and longing for culture and beauty among men. The father of Marxism is steam.

Old wives prophecy from coffee dregs. Karl Marx prophecied from steam.

What Marx considered to be similarity to socialism, the immediately preparatory stage prior to socialism, was nothing more than the organization of the production plant resulting from the technical requirements of the steam-engine within capitalism.

Thus two completely different forms of centralization met here: the economic centralization of capitalism, the rich man who concentrates as much money, as much labor as possible around himself, and the technical centralization of the industrial plant, the steam-engine, which must have the work machines and the working men close to itself as the power center, and therefore created the great manufacturing plants and refined the division of labor. As such, the economic centralization of capitalism — except for a few isolated cases — does not at all require centralization of the technical plant. Wherever human work-energy or simple, hand- or foot-driven machines are cheaper to use than the steam-engine, the capitalist prefers home industry scattered over the countryside in villages and farms over the factory. Thus it was the technical requirements of the steam-engine that produced the great factory-buildings and the large cities full of factories and rented tenements.

These two originally separate and completely different forms of centralization naturally combined and exercised the strong reciprocal influences. Capitalism made tremendously rapid advances through the steam-engine. However, capitalism with its technically centralized institutions, especially the concentration of workers mainly from the open country, a trend which is still accelerating to this day, hampers the electrical distribution of steam and water power, which by nature would have a decentralizing effect, from exercising this effect. Still it cannot be denied that this electrical transmission of energy has also produced capitalist exploitation of small separate workshops, as for instance in the knife-blade industry of Solingen, while simultaneously strengthening small industry and crafts in a positive way. In the future this potential will bring about a renewal of small industry and crafts and present broad opportunities for cooperative organizations to employ energy and motors.

This combination of the centralization of technology and capital then led to further highly intensive capitalist centralization: centralizations of commerce, banking, wholesale and retail trade, transportation, etc.

Yet a third centralization has, generally independently of the two others, prospered in our times: the centralization of the state bureaucracy and the military system. In addition to the huge factories and tenements, another group of huge buildings was erected in the large cities: the barracks of the bureaucrats, where in each of these public building's hundreds of small rooms, and in each drab room one, two or three green tables, and behind each green table sit one, two or three yawning minor officials with pen behind their ear and lunch-bag in hand; and the barracks of the soldiers, where thousands of strong young men must pass time in useless sport — sport ought to serve only as recreation after useful work — and are bored and engage in all kinds of sexual stupidities and obscenities.

With so much unculture, overcrowding, removal from the earth and culture, with so much waste of labor, overburdening with unproductive work and loafing around, so much senseless misery, resulting from all these forms of centralism, we find additional barracks of our time becoming increasingly numerous and large: the work-houses, jails and prisons, and the houses of prostitution.

When the Marxists deny that their doctrine is merely a product of technical centralization of enterprises we must in fact admit that all these forms of desolate, ugly, uniform, restrictive, and repressive centralism were, to a certain extent, exemplary for Marxism, and influenced its origin, development and propagation. Thus, it is not surprising that real Marxists are now found almost exclusively in countries dominated by the sergeant, the minor official and bureaucrat, namely, Prussia and Russia. The word "discipline" with its crude imperiousness is heard nowhere as often as in the Prussian army and German-Prussian Social Democracy. Nonetheless none of these centralizations is so constituted that it could produce a monstrosity that could really and truly be called "socialism" except the technical centralization of steam.

Never will socialism "blossom" from capitalism, as the unpoetic Marx so lyrically sang, but his doctrine and his party, Marxism and Social Democracy did develop from steam energy.

Watch how the workers and craftsmen and the sons and daughters of the peasants move away from the country, and are replaced by armies of migrant crop-pickers! Watch how every morning thousands upon thousands enter the factories and are spat out again in the evening!

"The same compulsion to work for all, the establishment of industrial armies, especially for agriculture," wrote Marx and Engels in *The Communist Manifesto*, not as a description and premonition of the coming splendors of capitalism, but as one of the measures they proposed "for the most advanced countries" as the beginning of their socialism—this sort of socialism certainly grows out of the undisturbed further development of capitalism!

Add to this, capitalist concentration which looked as if the number of capitalists and of fortunes would become ever fewer, add further the model of the omnipotent government in the centralized state of our times, and add finally the ever greater perfection of the industrial machines, the ever increased division of labor, the replacement of the trained craftsman by the unskilled machine-operator—all this however seen in an exaggerated and caricatured light, for it all has another side and is never a schematically unilinear development. It is a struggle and equilibrium of various tendencies, but everything Marxism sees is always grotesquely simplified and caricatured. Add finally the hope that work-hours will become shorter and shorter and human work more and more productive: then the state of the future is finished. The future state of the Marxists: the blossom on the tree of governmental, capitalist and technological centralization.

It must yet be added that the Marxist, when he dreams his pipe-dreams especially boldly—for never was a dream emptier and drier, and if there ever have been unimaginative fantasists, the Marxists are the worst—the Marxist extends his centralism and economic bureaucracy beyond present-day states and advocates a world organization to regulate and direct the production and distribution of goods. That is Marxism's internationalism. As formerly in the International everything was supposed to be regulated and decided by the London-based general council and today in Social Democracy all decisions are made in Berlin, this world production authority will someday look into every pot and will have the amount of grease for every machine listed in its ledger.

One more layer and our description of Marxism will be finished.

The forms of organization of what these people call socialism blossom forth completely in capitalism, except that these organizations, these ever expanding — through steam — factories are still in the hands of private entrepreneurs, exploiters. We have already seen, however, that they are supposed to be reduced to a smaller and smaller number by competition. One must visualize clearly what this means: first a hundred thousand — then a few thousand — then a few hundred — then some seventy or fifty — then a few absolutely monstrous giant entrepreneurs

Opposed to them stand the workers, the proletarians. They become more and more numerous, the middle classes disappear, and with the number of workers the number, intensity and power of the machines also grows, so that not only the number of workers, but also the number of unemployed, the so-called industrial reserve-armies, increases. According to this description, capitalism reaches an impasse and the struggle against it, i.e., against the few remaining capitalists, becomes easier and easier for the countless masses of disinherited who have an interest in change. Thus it must be remembered that in Marxist doctrine everything is immanent, though the term is taken from another area and misapplied. Here it means that nothing requires special efforts or mental insights, everything follows smoothly from the social process. The so-called socialist forms of organization are already immanent in capitalism. Similarly in the proletarians, their disinterestedness toward the existing conditions is immanent, i.e., the tendency to socialism, the revolutionary mentality, is an integrating element of the proletarians. The proletarians have nothing to lose; they have a world to gain!

How beautiful, how truly poetic is this statement (which stems neither from Marx nor from Engels) and how much truth it supposedly contains.

And yet the following statement is truer than the claim that the proletarians are born revolutionaries: the proletarians are the born uncultured plodders. The Marxist speaks so contemptuously of the petit-bourgeois, but every characteristic and habit of life that can be called petit-bourgeois is typical of the average proletarian, just as unfortunately even in jails and prisons most cells are occupied by uncultured plodders. With this "unfortunately" that slipped from my tongue, I of course by no means regret that the cultured men are free, but it is truly saddening for poor fools, victims of circumstances, who therefore had to break the legally established conventions, just as everything that happens in the world must happen, that this was not even a consequence of a rebellious mentality's replacing convention in the psyche. In fact, the convention, which they broke, lives in their temperment, in their opinions, and in the way they mishandle their fellow sufferers and sometimes even themselves, generally just as firmly as in most other men.

What we are speaking of here, the proletarian's uncultured mentality is, incidentally, one of the reasons why Marxism, systematized unculturedness, has been so well received by the proletariat. Only a very shallow veneer of the tongue with education is needed to transform an average proletarian without any exceptional qualities into a usable party-leader—and this is done fastest and cheapest in the poly-clinics called party-schools.

These and other party-leaders thus naturally adhere firmly to the Marxist doctrine that the proletariat is revolutionized by social necessity, at least the little bit still necessary to overcome capitalism, which after all consists of fewer and fewer persons and is becoming intrinsically more and more fragile. For in addition to the above-listed factors that lead to the inevitable collapse of capitalism, it contains another immanent peril: crises. As the program of German Social Democracy says in such beautiful and so genuinely Marxist terms (otherwise various ungenuine elements have crept in, which the makers of this program now are calling revisionist in their opponents): the powers of production are growing beyond the capacity of contemporary society. This contains the genuinely Marxist teaching that in contemporary society the forms of production have become more and more socialist and that these forms lack only the right form of ownership. They call it social ownership, but when they call the capitalist factory system a social production (not only Marx in *Capital* does this, but the present-day Social Democrats in their currently effective program call work in the forms of present-day capitalism, social work), we know the real implications of their socialist forms of labor. Just as they consider the production forms of steam technology in capitalism to be a socialist form of labor, so they consider the centralized state to be the social organization of society and bureaucratically administered state-property to be common property! These people really have no instinct for what society means. They haven't the least idea that society can only be a society of societies, only a federation, only freedom. They therefore do not know that socialism is anarchy and federation. They believe socialism is government, while others who thirst for culture want to create socialism because they want to escape from the disintegration and misery of capitalism and its concomitant poverty, spiritlessness and coercion, which is only the other side of economic individualism. In short, they want to escape from the state into a society of societies and voluntary association.

Because, as these Marxists say, socialism is still so to speak, the private property of the entrepreneurs, who produce wildly and senselessly, and since they are in possession of the socialist production powers (read: of steam power, perfected production machinery and the superfluously available proletarian masses), that is, because this situation is like a magic broomstick in the hands of the sorcerer's apprentice, a deluge of goods, overproduction and confusion must be the result, i.e., crises must ensue, which, no matter what the details may be, always come about, at least in the opinion of the Marxists, because the regulative function of a statistically controlling and directing world state authority is necessary to go with the socialist mode of production, which, in their wickedly stupid view, already exists. As long as this control authority is missing, "socialism" is still imperfect, and disorder must result. The forms of organization of capitalism are good, but they lack order, discipline, and strict centralization. Capitalism and government must come together, and where we would speak of state capitalism, those Marxists say that socialism is here. But just as their socialism contains all forms of capitalism and regimentation, and just as they allow the tendency to uniformity and leveling that exists today to progress to its ultimate perfection, the proletarian too is carried over into their socialism. The proletarian of the capitalist enterprise has become the state proletarian, and proletarianization has, when this type of socialism begins, really and predictably reached gigantic proportions. Everyone without exception is an employee of the state.

Capitalism and the state must come together — that is in truth Marxism's ideal. Although they do not want to hear of their ideal, we see they seek to promote this trend of development. They do not see that the tremendous power and bureaucratic desolation of the state is necessary only because our communal life has lost the spirit, because justice and love, the economic associations and the blossoming multiplicity of small social organisms have vanished. They see nothing of all this deep decay of our times; they hallucinate progress. Technology progresses, of course. It actually does so in many times of culture, although not always — there are also cultures without technical progress. It progresses especially in times of decay, of the individualization of spirit and the atomization of the masses. That is precisely our point. The real progress of technology together with the real baseness of the time is — to speak, for once, Marxistically for the Marxists — the real, material basis for the ideological superstructure, namely for the Marxists' Utopia of progressive socialism. However, since not only advancing technology is reflected in their little spirit but also the other tendencies of the time, capitalism too is progress in their eyes, and for them the centralized state is progress. It is not just irony that we are here applying the language of the so-called materialistic conception of history to the Marxists themselves. They took this conception of history from somewhere and now that we have gotten to know it we can say more clearly than before where they found it: namely completely in the own self. Yes indeed, what the Marxists say of the relationship of spiritual structures and thinking to the circumstances of the time is indeed true for all contemporaries, by which must be understood here all those who are only the child and expression of their time, uncreative, non-resistant, without any intrinsic foundations and spiritual personality. Again we have come to the uncultured plodder and the Marxist. For him it is quite true that his ideology is only the superstructure of the evil of our time. In times of decay there does in fact prevail an un-spirit that is the expression of the time, and so today the Marxists predominate. They cannot know that times of culture and fulfillment cannot develop out of the times of decline — which they call progress — but they come from the spirit of those who in their nature never belonged to their time. They cannot know and understand that what will be called history in the great periods of change is achieved neither by uncultured and docile contemporaries, nor by social processes, but by isolated and solitary men, who are isolated precisely because folk and community are at home in them and have fled both to them and with them.

No doubt, the Marxists believe that if the front and back sides of our degradation, the capitalist conditions of production and the state, were brought together, then their progress and development would have reached its goal and so justice and equality would be established. Their comprehensive economic state, whether it be the heir to previous states or their world state, is a republican and democratic structure, and they really believe that the laws of such a state would provide for the welfare of all the common people, since they comprise the state. Here we must be allowed to burst out in irrepressible laughter at this most pitiful of all stodgy fantasies. Such a complete mirror image of the Utopia of the sated bourgeois can in fact only be the product of undisturbed laboratory development of capitalism. We will waste no more time on this accomplished ideal of the era of decline and of depersonalized unculture, this government of dwarves. We will see that true culture is not empty but fulfilled and that the true society is a multiplicity of real, small affinities that grow out of the binding qualities of individuals, out of the spirit, a structure of communities, and a union. This "socialism" of the Marxists is a gigantic goiter that supposedly will develop. Never fear, we will soon see that it will not develop. Our socialism, however, should grow in the hearts of men. It wishes to cause the hearts of those who belong together to grow in unity and spirit. The alternative is not pigmy-socialism or socialism of the spirit, for we will soon see that if the masses follow the Marxists or even the revisionists, then capitalism will remain. It absolutely does not tend to change suddenly into the "socialism" of the Marxists nor to develop into the socialism of the revisionists, which can be thus called only with a shy voice. Decline — in our case, capitalism — has in our time just as much vitality as culture and expansion had in other times. Decline does not at all mean decrepitude, a tendency toward collapse or drastic reversal. Decline, the Epoch of sunkenness, folklessness, spiritlessness, is capable of lasting for centuries or millennia. Decline, in our case, capitalism, possesses in our time precisely that measure of vitality which is not found in contemporary culture and expansion. It has as much strength and energy as we fail to muster for socialism. The choice we face is not: one form of socialism, or the other, but simply: capitalism or socialism; the state of society; unspirit or spirit. The doctrine of Marxism does not lead out of capitalism. Nor is there any truth to Marxism's doctrine that capitalism can at times out-trump Baron Münchhausen's fantastic accomplishment of pulling himself out of a strange swamp by his pig-tail, i.e., the prophecy that capitalism will emerge out of its own swamp by virtue of its own development.

Later we will have to show in greater detail how false this doctrine is. To show that capitalism does not have the immanent tendency to develop to any form of socialism, we now need merely to rid ourselves of the monstrosity, the ugly thing that the Marxists call socialism. Capitalism develops neither into this nor into any kind of socialism. To show this, we must answer some questions.

Let us, then, ask: is it true that society is as the Marxists portray it? that its further development is, or must be, or even probably will be so? Is it true that the capitalists are devouring one another, until finally there will be only one gigantic capitalist? Is it true? or should there be only one capitalist? Is it true that the middle classes are disappearing, that proletarization is without exception increasing rapidly and that an end to the process can be foreseen? That unemployment is becoming worse and worse and that therefore such circumstances cannot continue to exist? And is there a spiritual influence on the disinherited, so that they must, with natural necessity, rise up, revolt, become revolutionary? Is it, finally, true that the crises are becoming more and more comprehensive and devastating? that capitalism's productive capacity is outgrowing it and must therefore grow into so-called socialism?

Is all that true? What is really the situation as regards this entire complex of observations, warnings, threats and prophecies?

These are the questions we must now ask, and which we have always been asking, we anarchists namely, from the beginning, as long as Marxism has existed. Long before Marxism existed there was a real socialism, especially the socialism of the greatest socialist, Pierre Joseph Proudhon, and it was afterwards overshadowed by Marxism, but we are bringing it back to life. Those are our questions, and they are the questions which, from a very different perspective, the revisionists also pose.

Only after we have answered these questions, which we have touched upon here and there in our description of Marxism, and have contrasted the real picture of our conditions and course which capitalism has taken until now, especially since the appearance of the *Communist Manifesto* and *Capital*, with the *zeit*-ideological simplification and dialectical caricature of Marxism, can we proceed to say what our socialism and our road to socialism is. For socialism — let it be said immediately and the Marxists ought to hear it, as long as the wisps of fog of their own obtuse theory of progress are still in the air — does not depend for its possibility on any form of technology and satisfaction of needs. Socialism is possible at all times, if enough people want it. But it will always look different, start and progress differently, depending on the level of available technology, i.e., also of the number of people who begin it and the means they contribute or have inherited from the past — nothing begins from nothing. Therefore, as was said above: no depiction of an ideal, no description of a Utopia is given here. First, we must examine our conditions and spiritual temperaments more clearly. Only then can we say to what kind of socialism we are called, to what type of men we are speaking. Socialism, you Marxists, is possible at all times and with any kind of technology. It is possible for the right people at all times, even with very primitive technology, while at all times, even with splendidly developed machine technology it is impossible for the wrong group. We know of no development that must bring it. We know of no such necessity as a natural law. Now therefore we will show that these our times and our capitalism that has blossomed as far as Marxism are by no means as you say they are. Capitalism will not necessarily change into socialism. It need not perish. Socialism will not necessarily come, nor must the capital-state-proletariat-socialism of Marxism come and that is not too bad. In fact no socialism at all *must* come — that will now be shown.

Yet socialism *can* come and *should* come — if we *want* it, if we create it — that too will be shown.

5.

The Marxists claim:

1. Capitalist concentration in industry, in trade, in the monetary and credit system is a preliminary state, the beginning of socialism.

2. The number of capitalist entrepreneurs — or at least of capitalist companies — is decreasing constantly; the size of individual companies is expanding; the middle class is shrinking and is doomed to extinction; the number of proletarians is growing immeasurably.

3. The quantity of these proletarians is always so great that there must always be unemployed among them; this industrial reserve army depresses the circumstances of life; over-production results because more is produced than can be consumed. Thus, period crises are inescapable.

4. The disproportion between tremendous wealth in the hands of a few and poverty and insecurity for the masses will ultimately become so great that a terrible crisis will result and the dissatisfaction of the masses will become so intensified that a catastrophe, a revolution must come, in the course of which capitalist ownership can and must be transformed into social ownership.

These main tenets of Marxism have often been criticized by anarchist, bourgeois, and recently by revisionist scholars. Whether one is glad or sorry, all the same, in honesty we must admit the accuracy of the following results of the critique.

One ought not to speak of capitalist entrepreneurs under the assumption that the existence of capitalist society depends particularly on their number. Rather one ought to speak of how many have a stake in capitalism, of those who, as regards their external livelihood, enjoy relative prosperity and security under capitalism. It is a matter for those who have a stake in capitalism and in general, despite exceptions, are dependent on capitalism for their opinions, strivings and moods, regardless of whether they are independent entrepreneurs, agents with good positions, higher officials or employees, stockholders, pensioners, or whatever. Here, on the basis of tax data and other incontrovertible observations, it can only be said that the number of these persons has not decreased, but has increased somewhat both absolutely and relatively.

Especially in this field one must avoid being led by emotions and drawing general conclusions from small personal experiences and partial observations. Everyone can, of course, see that the chain stores, and in some places the consumers' cooperatives are busily eliminating the small and medium-sized merchants. Nor must only the merchants who are ruined and forced out of business be considered, but far more those who do not have the courage and means to become independent. The question is only where a great part of these non-independents is to be classified, namely whether they are proletarians. This topic will be treated directly below when we investigate the concept "proletarians." Despite all such personal experiences and individual perceptions of an amateur nature, it cannot be denied that the number of those with a stake in capitalism is by no means decreasing, but it is actually increasing.

As for the number of capitalist companies, it can be granted that it is decreasing. However, it must be added that this decrease is slow and insignificant and shows no tendency to rapid progression, so that the end of capitalism, if it really is supposed to depend on this decrease, would still not be foreseeable for thousands of years.

The question of the new middle class has often been dealt with. Its existence cannot be denied. No one has ever written that middle class can mean only independent craftsmen, merchants, small farmers and pensioners.

We can link the question: Who belongs to the middle class? with the other one: Who is a proletarian? The Marxists insist with all their might, as if clinging to a last safety line, that: a member of the owning class is independent, owns his own tools and has his own clientele, while a proletarian is everyone who is dependent, does not own his own tools and is not independent of the purchasers of his goods or services. This explanation is no longer sufficient and it leads to quite grotesque results. Years ago in a public meeting in one of the largest halls in Berlin, I debated this aspect of the question with Clara Zetkin and I asked her if the owner of the hall was probably, like most owners of such establishments, completely dependent on the brewery that delivers his beer. This brewery holds a mortage on his place, he is obliged for years ahead to serve only their beer and the tables, chairs, glasses are the property of the brewery. His income comprises, year after year, 30,000, 40,000 or 50,000 Marks. In this capitalist age, functions have arisen for which the customary terms no longer are adequate. He is neither employee nor agent, but he is not independent and is not the owner of his means of labor. Is he a proletarian? — Not everyone will want to believe it, but in fact the answer I got was: yes, he is a proletarian. It could not be a question of standard of living, nor of social position, but only of the ownership of the instruments of labor and security. The existence of this man deprived of his means of labor was quite insecure.

I had at that time allowed myself to say, quite simply and not really in scientific language, that a proletarian is whoever earns a proletarian standard of living. There are, of course, all possible gradations from the greatest misery, via an existence always bordering on the bare minimum, to the worker who can live with his family, come what may, surviving times of unemployment, while unknowingly, shortening his life through undernourishment or at least impairing his own vitality and that of his offspring and never attaining a modest surplus income without which participation in art, beauty, free merriment is not possible. This is how the word "proletarian" is generally understood and how we will use it. But even the Marxists really use it this way, and they cannot do otherwise. Only these proletarians have no stake in capitalism and are interested in changing conditions (namely when they grasp their interests from the viewpoint of the whole society). Only to these proletarians does the statement apply that they have nothing to lose but their chains, and they have a world to gain.

Even in the upper strata of the working force, there are professions that no longer belong completely to the proletariat. Some categories of workers in the book trade, some construction workers would, despite their relatively high wages and favorable working hours, still have to be classified among the proletarians because of the great insecurity of their position and the constant threat of unemployment, except that through their own institutions, in their unions, which have inestimable value for security of life within capitalism, they have provided themselves with a means to survive these periods tolerably well. But it must be admitted that this is a borderline example; and because of the danger of not being sufficiently protected from destitution in cases of accident, injury or old-age, they can still be ranked as proletarians.

On the other hand, it must be said that in other strata there are men who live in bitter poverty but still ought not to be called proletarians. Among these are poor writers and artists, doctors, military officers, and the like. Under harsh deprivations, they or their parents have often assured themselves of a form of culture which often does not protect them from hunger or stale bread or a dish in the soup-line. Yet through their external living habits and their inner wealth they differ from the proletarians and constitute, whether they are solitary, lead an orderly or a wild life, a class by themselves, which, incidentally, seems to be increasing faster than the great proletariat. A few of them, if they have lost their inner grip, sometimes sink into the lowest strata of the proletariat, becoming bums, vagabonds, pimps, swindlers, or habitual criminals.

However, among the broad ranks of those who are dependent in any form, there are very many who are not at all proletarians. No doubt, for instance, among employees in stores, e.g., there are many who differ from the proletariat neither physically nor mentally. The same is true of many draftsmen, technicians, and the like. Lower officials again are a category by themselves; from a psychological point of view, they should be called slaves rather than proletarians. Let us not resolve to what category party officials and union officials belong. They have to be considered more for their influence than for their number.

Now we have a large, actually increasing number of people who, no doubt, comprise a new middle class, unless they belong to the wealthy group. For instance, store employees, branch and section managers, directors, engineers and top engineers, agents, salesmen, etc. Their role in capitalism is such that neither their proletarianization nor their revolutionizing will result from their material situation and the corresponding attitude. However, only such "proletarians" can come under consideration for Marxism. The fact that there are exceptional men or masses of exceptional men with an exceptional mentality, so that it is no longer a matter of a direct and mechanical relationship of attitude and will to the external situation, is precisely what Marxism ignores and what we must re-emphasize.

But what about insecurity? It must be noted that insecurity exists for all members of capitalist society, but we have to distinguish the degree of it. For we are speaking of certain strata that have a particular interest in capitalism and call them, for short, capitalists, whereas in truth we all, without the least exception, as long as capitalism exists, have a share in it, are interwoven with it and in truth are capitalistically active, including the proletarians. So we must, even with regard to security, make loose distinctions and draw only flexible boundaries, since we are dealing not with abstract structures, but with historically given realities. For the many whom we must rank in the middle class among the propertied strata, although they do not dispose over their own means of labor and clientele, insecurity is normally only a theoretical possibility, and is an exception in practice. But since the Marxists in fact do not split hairs and set up concepts, but attempt to predict the destiny and behavior of certain strata in an apparently scientific language, they ought not — unless they prefer to deceive themselves and their own wishes and defend false theories to the end, despite all elucidations — to deny that there is a very considerable, slowly growing number of men who are dependent and without their own means of labor, yet who, all things considered, will never run the danger of becoming proletarians.

Thus it already seems that the prophecies of the Marxists are in bad shape. And yet it must be conceded: they were once as true as any prophetic pronouncement can be. Karl Marx, although he used genuine prophetic and poetic language only in rare moments of elation, and usually employed scientific language and not rarely scientific mystification, was a real prophet in the days when he first formed and expressed his ideas on the basis of his observation of the early years of capitalism. But that means: he was a warner. He announced the future which would have come if what he saw before his eyes continued on the same course. He was a prophet in yet another respect too, not only as a warner, but as a man of influence, for he himself played a great role in preventing what he saw from staying the way it was, for his warnings took effect and changes were made. His words said, without his knowing it: You capitalists, if this mad exploitation, this rapid proletarization and wild competition among yourselves keep on, if you continue devouring one another, pushing one another into the proletariat, consolidating enterprises, lessening the number of companies, increasing the size of each one, then everything must come to a quick end!

But things did not go on that way. Capitalism has created such a widely ramified multiplicity of needs, satisfied so much expensive, medium-priced, cheap and trashy luxury, while the big industries have given birth to such a need for supporting industries, that consequently no form of technology has become dispensable, entire new jobs, e.g., home and village industries, small and medium-sized factories have arisen, and even the number of door-to-door salesmen and representatives has not diminished, while specialized shops, though small and medium-sized shops are forced out of many fields, find new possibilities elsewhere in others in exchange.

The struggle of competition has by no means always followed the abstract schema or poetically heightened despair. We are still in the midst of the great movement of consolidation into trusts and syndicates, which unquestionably does deprive many small firms of their customers and existence, but also enables many moderate-sized, large and very large companies to recognize and protect their mutual interests in alliance against the consumers, instead of ruining themselves in a merciless race for consumers. We also see small tradesmen learning from them and forming their own associations and cooperatives in order to survive. The associations of independent cabinet-makers have their large display-rooms and compete with big firms. Small merchants join together in purchasing-groups or agree on price-fixing. Capitalism everywhere preserves its vitality, and instead of its forms leading to socialism, on the contrary it uses the genuinely socialist form of the cooperative, of mutual cooperation, for its purposes of exploiting the consumers and monopolizing the market.

The state, by its legislation, has also seen to it that capitalism remains healthy and strong in the various countries. As the syndicates within one country see to it that undercutting does not take place and unfair competition is restricted, tariff-policy prevents the capitalism of one country from destroying that of another. The tendency of national tariff-legislation and international agreements is to provide increasingly equal opportunities in the world market. This equality of trading opportunities was only apparently provided in the system of free trade, for the populations, wage conditions, civilizations, technologies, natural conditions, prices and quantities of available resources are not the same in the various countries. Tariff-policy has the tendency to counterbalance real inequalities by artificial regulations. This is only in its beginnings. For the moment, activity in this area is still barbaric. Each state still seeks to exploit its momentary power, but the direction of this tendency is in any case clear.

Moreover, the state has also seen to it in more or less all other areas that the worst excesses of capitalism are removed. This is called social policy. Unquestionably the laws protecting workers against the worst excesses of capitalism, such as the exploitation of children and juveniles, have created certain safeguards. In other ways, state intervention, regulation and provision have improved the situation of the proletarians in capitalism and thus have improved capitalism's own situation. Social security laws, especially in cases of illness, have had the same effect.

But the moral results of this legislation were even more important for capitalism than these actual effects. Both for the masses of proletarians and for the politicians, it has blurred the difference between their future government and their present one. The state acquired for itself and its police a new sphere of power: inspection of factories, mediation between worker and enterprisers, the care of sick, aged, retired proletarians, protection not only against occupational hazards but also against those of a dependent and insecure position. The patriarchal attitude of the state, childish confidence in the state and its laws on the part of citizens have been strengthened and increased. The revolutionary mood in the masses and in the political parties has been essentially weakened.

What both entrepreneurs themselves and the state undertook, was continued by the proletarians, not only in their political collaboration in governmental legislation, but also through institutions which they created in their own solidarity. Not without reason did Marx and Engels originally want to have nothing to do with the trade unions. They considered these professional organizations useless, harmful relics of the petit-bourgeois age. They also probably sensed what role the solidarity of the workers as producers might some day play in stabilizing and preserving capitalism. They could not stop the workers from not acting as the destiny-chosen redeemers and accomplishers of socialism, but as if they only had one life which they are forced to live under capitalism and which they must for better or worse shape as well as they can. Thus the workers too, through their union fund, protect themselves against hardship in case of unemployment, change of residence, illness, sometimes age and sudden death. They provide for rapid procurement of jobs suited to their interests, wherever they can hold their own against the requirements of the entrepreneurs, the municipalities, or private employment agencies. They have begun, by wage-contracts binding on both parties for longer periods, to create secure relationships between entrepreneurs and workers. They have let themselves be driven by the reality and requirements of the present and could not be restrained from doing so by any theories or party programs. Rather, the party programs and theories had to follow the means of information created by the reality of the capitalist working conditions. All sorts of doctrinaires and idealists, from various camps, want to prevent the workers from providing for their pitifully desolate present life by purposeful measures. That, of course, cannot succeed. The workers, in masses, like to be called the revolutionary class with flattering and adoring words, but that does not make them revolutionaries. Revolutionaries exist in masses only when there is a revolution. One of the Marxists' worst errors, whether they call themselves Social Democrats or anarchists, is the opinion that a revolution could be achieved by means of revolutionaries, whereas the reverse it true: revolutionaries come into existence only by means of the revolution. To seek to create, multiply and assemble revolutionaries for a few decades in order to be sure to have the right number of them in case of a revolution is a typically German, childishly pedantic and impractical idea. There is no need to fear a lack of revolutionaries: they actually arise by a sort of spontaneous generation—namely when the revolution comes. But for the revolution, a new formative power, to come, new conditions must be created. They can best be created by impartial men, who might well be called optimists (although it need not be so), by men who do not consider it certain that the revolution must come, but who are so deeply convinced of the necessity and justice of their new cause that they do not regard the obstacles and dangers as insurmountable and inevitable. Such men do not want revolution, which is at best a means; rather, they seek a certain reality, which is their goal. Historical memories can have bad effects, if for instance men pose as ancient Romans or Jacobins, while they have quite other tasks to perform, but even worse is the sort of historical science which Hegelianized Marxism has brought. Who knows how long ago we would already have had the revolution behind us, if we had never given a thought to the coming one. Marxism has brought us a kind of step that is reminiscent of nothing, not even of the Echternach leaping procession, in which each person always jumps two steps forward and one backward, which at least results in some forward motion. Marxism makes intentional apparent motions toward the goal of revolution but thereby moves only further and further away from it. It turns out that envisaging the revolution in its result always is equivalent to fear of it. It is advisable in one's actions not to think of what could happen, but of what one must do. The demand of the day must be fulfilled by precisely those who want to construct the work of their heart, their desire, their justice and their imagination very fundamentally and radically.

Of course they must build quite differently from the patching up of capitalism as we have observed it in these last decades undertaken by the entrepreneurs, the state and the workers themselves, as briefly described above.

The workers' struggle in their organizations, the trade unions, to improve their situation in life and their working conditions is also a part of this context. We have seen how the workers in their capacity as producers interfere in and regulate what the Marxists call an unavertable destiny though their union fund system. However another important task of the unions is still the struggle for higher wages and the shortening of working hours by negotiations and strikes.

The struggle to raise wages is always really a struggle of individual producers, however many and united, against the totality of consumers. Since everyone at some time or other enters this producers' struggle, it is a struggle of the workers against themselves. The workers and their organizations are inclined, in a thoroughly amateurish way, to consider the money, the wages they receive as an absolute quantity. There is no doubt that 5 Marks is more than 3 Marks. Of course we cannot begrudge or fail to understand the worker's joy that while yesterday he received only 3 Marks, from today on he will receive 5 Marks per day in wages. The question is only whether in three, five or ten years he will still have reason to rejoice. For money is only the expression of the relationships of prices and wages to one another. It all depends on the purchasing power of money.

Of course, the raising of wages, just like of taxes and tariffs, causes the prices of commodities to go up. Naturally the piano-worker is inclined to argue as follows: What do I care if pianos have become more expensive! I get higher wages and I don't buy a piano, but bread, meat, clothes, and housing, etc. Even the weavers, for example, can say: Though the material I must buy becomes more expensive, I have made only a small portion of my needs more expensive, but I have increased my entire wages with which to cover my total needs.

The answer to this and similar objections of private egoism can be given immediately in the fundamental, comprehensive form we owe to P.J. Proudhon: "What is considered true in economic matters for the ordinary private person, becomes false the moment one seeks to apply it to the whole society."

The workers, in their wage struggles, act just as participants of capitalist society must act: as egoists fighting with their elbows and, since they can accomplish nothing alone, they fight as organized, united egoists. Organized and united they are comrades of one branch of the economy. All these branch-associations together comprise the totality of the workers in their role as producers for the capitalist commodity market. In this role they carry on a struggle, so they think, against the capitalist enterprisers, but in reality against themselves in their capacity as consumers.

The so-called capitalist is not a fixed, tangible figure. He is an intermediary, on whom of course much of the blame can be laid, but the blows the worker as producer seeks militantly to inflict upon him miss the mark. The worker hits and hits, but he is striking as if at an intangible mirage and his blows fall back on himself.

In the struggles within capitalism only those who fight as capitalists can win real victories, i.e., achieve permanent advantages. If an engineer, a director, or a sales employee is indispensable to his employer because of his personal skill or his knowledge of company secrets, then he can one day say: Until now I received 20,000 Marks salary, give me 100,000 or I will go over to the competition! If he succeeds in this, then he has perhaps achieved a final victory for the rest of his life. He acted as a capitalist. He fought egoism with egoism. So an individual worker can sometimes make himself indispensable, improve his situation in life, or enter completely into an area of wealth. But as the workers struggle in their trade unions, they reduce themselves to numbers, each of which is personally insignificant. They thus accept their role as cogs in the machine. They act only as parts of a whole, and the whole reacts against them.

Thus the workers in their struggle as producers cause the production of all articles to become more expensive. This inflation, even though it affects in part luxury articles, results mainly in a price-rise of articles of necessary mass need. In fact not in a proportionate price-rise, but in a disproportionate one. When wages are increased, prices go up disproportionately; when wages are decreased, however, the prices fall disproportionately slowly and slightly.

The result is that over a period of time the worker's struggle in his role as a producer harms the workers in their reality as consumers.

This does not in the least mean that the unusual inflation in the cost of living, which makes life more difficult for many, can be blamed entirely or mainly of the workers themselves. Many causes are involved and egoism is always at fault, for it knows no general economy and therefore no culture. One of these factors was the struggle of the producers, who in this struggle expressly consented to become members of capitalism, though at its lowest level. Everything that the capitalists do as capitalists is base; what the workers do as capitalists is proletarianly base. Of course, this means only that they have accepted a vile role. It does not change the fact that in and out of this role they can be decent, bold, noble, heroic. Even robbers, can be heroic, but the workers in their struggle for wage and price increases are robbers without knowing it, robbers of their own selves.

Someone will point out that the unions, with strikes, fight not only for wage-increases but also for shortening of working hours, solidarity with other workers' grievances, work credentials, etc.

The answer to this is that in this context the only relevant effect is the wage-increase and that it would be a gross misunderstanding to think that we are here waging a fight against the unions! Oh no! It is recognized here that the unions are a completely necessary organization within capitalism. Let it finally be understood, what is really being said here. It is recognized here that the workers are not a revolutionary class, but a bunch of poor wretches who must live and die under capitalism. It is admitted here that the "social policy" of the state, the municipalities, the proletarian policies of the labor party, the proletarian struggle of the labor unions, and the union fund are all necessities for the workers. It is also conceded that the poor workers are not always able to respect the interests of the whole, even of the whole laboring force. The various economic sectors must wage their egoistic struggle, for every sector is a minority with respect to the others and must defend itself in view of the rising inflaton of the cost of living.

But everything that is recognized, admitted and conceded here, is a blow against Marxism, which seeks to understand the workers in their role as producers not as the poor lowest stage of capitalism, but as the destiny-chosen bearers of the revolution and of socialism.

Here I say: no! All these things are necessary under capitalism, as long as the workers do not understand how to get out of capitalism. But all this only leads around and around within the vicious circle of capitalism. Whatever happens within capitalist production can only lead deeper and deeper into it, but never out of it.

Let us look at the same thing once again briefly from another aspect. The capitalist — as Marx and others have shown extensively and in many valuable detailed descriptions — commit extortion against the workers; you have, their actions say, no means of labor, no workplace and means of enterprise, you exist in great numbers, often more than we need: therefore you must work for the wage we offer. As long as the capitalists, without needing an explicit agreement, simply act alike in this behavior toward the workers, but are locked in severe competition against one another nationally and internationally, two series of facts result from this: low wages and low prices. But if the workers unite and reply to this extortion, of necessity and rightfully: We all will not work if you refuse to pay higher wages; then the result is: higher wages and higher prices. If now the capitalists in turn unite, first for mutual support and security against the pressure of the workers, secondly, into cartels for price-fixing, then it becomes even harder and harder to raise wages, but easier and easier to raise prices. Next comes tariff-protection against cheap foreign competition. Sometimes even the importation of cheap, undemanding workers from foreign countries, or at least from rural areas, or the replacement of male workers by females, of skilled workers by unskilled, of hand labor by machines will follow. As can be seen, capitalism always has the advantage, as long as the workers can influence only wages but not also prices.

If therefore the workers retain their role as producers for the capitalist commodity market, but nonetheless want to radically improve their situation, i.e., take a part of capital's profits for themselves, then they have no choice but to aim, as much as possible, for wages and at the same time for low prices. By means of self-help they can, to a certain degree, move in this direction even within capitalism: if they place a socialistic form of organization, the cooperative, in the service of their consumption and thus eliminate a part of the middlemen from a portion of their needs in life—in the areas of food, dwelling, clothing, household goods, etc. Thus the workers, organized into unions, with relatively high wages, have a chance to really enjoy a part of their successes, when they fill their needs at relatively low prices in their consumer cooperatives (including housing cooperatives).

Another more radical way of transfering a part of capitalist profits into the hands of the workers, i.e., of confiscation of wealth, is the simultaneous setting of minimal wages and maximal prices by state or municipal legislation. That was the means of the medieval communes and was also—without real success—more proposed than really tried in the French revolution. Let us disregard the communal policies of the Middle Ages, where conditions were completely different and there was real culture and community, so-to-speak. Such confiscation of wealth is revolutionary class politics, which is recommendable temporarily perhaps in times of violent transition, but is at most just a small step on the road to socialism, not socialism itself, for socialism is precisely not a violent operation, but permanent health.

In both courses—the combination of union wages and cooperative prices and the simultaneous legislative fixing of high wages and low prices—there is an amateurish and only transitional amalgamation of capitalism and socialism. The organization of consumption is a beginning of socialism; the struggle of producers is a symptom of the decay of capitalism. High wages and low prices simultaneously are an alarming incongruency, and a capitalist society could not survive the simultaneous effect of a strong union movement and a solid consumer-cooperative movement any more than governmental imposition of high wages and low prices.

Such a fixed value of money—in both cases that is what we would have—would build up to a terrible explosion and be the beginning of the bankruptcy of the state and of society.

This could be the signal for violent revolution, but of course once again capitalism would save its skin. We can see even today how the union and cooperative movements are looked at askance. The unions are always the element of revolutionary unrest and have the inherent tendency to call a general strike. The cooperatives are a first step, however modest and unconscious, toward socialism. If these two movements were to become stronger and more aggressive and become aware of their complementariness, then so suffocating a paralysis of the economy would threaten, that an escape valve would have to be opened and the coalition in both economic areas would be restricted or completely prohibited.

No society can exist with high wages and low prices, nor with low wages and high prices. In times of relative peace, capitalists and workers in their blind private egoism will not refrain from seeking high prices and high salaries and wages and thus proliferating greed for luxury and dissatisfaction, displeasure with life, difficulties of obtaining money, work-stoppages, chronic crises and recession. At the time of the revolution, the trend will be, as Proudhon in 1848 so splendidly, though unsuccessfully, advocated: low prices! low income! low wages! and hopefully this time this idea will win out. It would result in freedom, mobility, a joyful mood, faster circulation of money, an easier life, modest joys, and simple innocence.

Incidentally, the prediction as to what the state and capitalism would do and would have to do, if they were pressed by the enormous combination of strong producer and consumer movements, must not be understood as a warning to the workers, in the familiar pattern of: "What can we do now? The state will forbid it!" Such a warning is not our way and our duty. Still we suppose that others will act according to their role; that is to be expected and need not bother us. Thus whoever believes he has a duty to see to it that capitalists earn less and less from workers and pay more and more to the workers has learned from us that a strong consumer-organization combined with a successful union struggle is the appropriate weapon. For hardly anyone will place much hope in the alternative, governmental wage-and-price fixing, and just as little in the related attempt to confiscate the excess income of the capitalist by an income tax in order to channel this excess via, for example, worker associations, to the proletariat. That is also a merely revolutionary method, incompetent and amateurish, and could be resorted to only very temporarily in a transition stage. Similar means were tried here and there without success under the French revolutionary government and were also recommended soon after 1848 by Girardin in France. Lasalle's political activity and program also moved in this direction.

Thus, we do not warn against the peculiar attempt to bring society to a halt by a combination of revolution and socialism, struggle and construction. We must only say that we are today far from that point and that the consumer cooperatives, as they exist today — though without knowing if they are only a pitiful beginning of socialism — are not the least suited to seriously ruining capitalism's prices or taking away their customers. Thus, this is the main duty of those who call for socialism. Socialism, if it is to come, must and can begin only with consumption.

This will be explained below. Here the task was to show that all one-sided struggle and all activity in the area of capitalist production, and so all action by the producers is a part of the history of capitalism and nothing more.

But since we have described and criticized the union activity of the producers, the workers' economic self-help, and the pressure they exert on the state for legislative regulations, two further important tasks of these organizatons and their struggles must be dealt with briefly. The main tasks of the unions still include the shortening of working hours and a change in the wage structure that is closely connected therewith, namely the replacement of piece work and contracted work by daily pay. Piece work and contracted work is payment for work according to the quantity and quality of the achieved product. It must be said that a just exchange system will always return to this type of payment for labor, but in a society of injustice against man, of neglect of his essential needs there can be hardly anything worse than the sharpening of the injustice against men by justice toward things. Under the rule of capitalism the worker cannot bear to have any other principle determine his income but his need. But since it is vitally necessary for him not only to earn enough for himself and his family to exist, but also not to ruin his health, sleep and leisure by long working hours, the struggle to shorten working hours also gives him a new reason to oppose piece work and contracted work. Shortened hours are not supposed to decrease his income and force him to an immeasurable increase in the intensity of work. Therefore it is also of dubious value that in some professions, e.g., in the construction trade, not a daily but an hourly wage is paid. This forces the workers in every fight for shorter working time to simultaneously battle for a higher hourly wage, and often such a dispute ends with a compromise; they achieve one objective and have to give up on the other. Thus, for example, they shorten their work day but at the same time curtail their real income. Therefore, everywhere under the capitalist system, the workers would have to oppose not only piece work and contracted work but also the hourly wage. A daily wage must be the demand of the capitalist worker. It expresses for everyone with an ear for the voice of culture or depravity, sharply and distinctly, that the worker is not a free man entering the market of life and exchanging goods, but that he is a slave whose subsistence must be granted by his master and guaranteed by society. Under the system of daily wages there is no outspoken relationship of work to the quantity and quality of its products, there is no *quid pro quo* exchange. There is only need that desires subsistence. Thus we again find that in the capitalist world the worker must defend a capitalist, anticultural institution to preserve his existence. Need and his role as a producer make him a servant and vassal of capitalism. The struggle of organized labor for its own daily wage system has its counterpart in the life of the state, i.e., in the struggle of the politically militant worker for the secret ballot. As undignified as it is to receive life sustenance in the form of a daily subsistence wage instead of exchanging product for product, i.e., receiving the price or wage for the product, it is equally pitiful to exercise one's right and duty toward the community in hiding, in the voting booth, out of fear. That was the reason why Egidy advocated public voting: he claimed that it could have no bad consequences for free and upright men. But that was a quixotic idea of a noble man. In our times the worker must seek to be a daily-wage-earner and the citizen must seek to be a timid helot. It is impossible to want to begin the cure at the individual level, where the inextricable symptoms of the capitalist economy and the capitalist state are exhibited. The worker must protect his life, and his life would be threatened if he did not go to vote in a closed booth, while his livelihood would be threatened if he did not receive a daily wage. All this and everything we are speaking of here are necessities of life as long as we do not abandon capitalism, but, of course, they are far from being ways and means of socialism.

Shortening the working hours has two sides, one of which is often alluded to, while not much attention is, as far as I know, paid to the other. It is, firstly, necessary to shorten the working time so that the worker can maintain his strength. It is not our task here to attack the unions — a necessary institution of struggle and regulation under capitalism — for that would, certainly be foolish, and almost criminal, because for the sake of the welfare of living men, not every single aspect of capitalism will be opposed. While we offer cool and objective criticism, we must pause for a moment to express deserved thanks to the unions for their important work. In all countries, they have shortened the workers' time of toil, of work at things that often did not interest them, in factories that made them tired and depressed, with extremely intensive techniques that rendered their activity spiritless and mortally boring. Thanks and praise to them; how many people have they provided with the occasion for rest after work-hours, for a beautiful family life, for the cheaply available joys of life, beautiful books and writings, and for participation in public life. How many — and how few! Only in recent years has a beginning been made, and mostly with inadequate, often with ridiculously bleak and party-political means, also to do something for the right use of the acquired leisure hours. Together with the struggle against the long work-hours, the unions out to fight against the devastations of alcoholism. They ought to regard it as their duty to concern themselves not only with the productive worker but also with the worker in his periods of rest after work. A lot still has to be done in this area, and there is much occasion for cooperation with artists, poets, and thinkers among our people. We ought not only to call for socialism. We ought not only to follow the voice of the idea and to build into the future. For the sake of the spirit that wants to become body and form for us, we must turn our attention to the living men of our people, the adults and children, and do our best so that their body and their spirit will be strong and fine, firm and supple. And then with these living men forward to socialism! But let this not be misunderstood as meaning that we ought to provide them with any particular, so-called socialist art or science or education. Alas, what mischief is carried on in this regard with party pamphlets and tendentious writing and how much more valuable, natural and free is, for example, so-called bourgeois science than the Social Democratic one! All such attempts lead to official, doctrinare bureaucracy. It is a great error, which all Marxist schools, Social Democratic as well as anarchist, share, that in working-class circles everything silent and eternal is despised or not known, while agitation and the superficial slogans of the day are overestimated and flourish crassly. Recently in a larger German city where I gave ten lectures on German literature, which were sponsored by a Social Democratic association and attended by members of the labor union, I myself experienced how after a lecture anarchist workers came into the hall which they had previously avoided to ask me to please give them a lecture sometime! At that time I decided to give them the following answer: I gave a lecture in which I spoke on Goethe, on Hölderlin and Novalis, on Stifter and Hebbel, on Dehmel and Liliencron and Heinrich van Reder and Christian Wagner, and many others; but you did not want to hear it, because you did not know that the voice of human beauty that is to come to us, the strong and calm rhythm and harmony of life is not to be found in the noise of the storm any more than in the gentle movement of rested breezes and the sacred stillness of immobility. "The blowing breeze, the trickling water, the growing grain, the billowing sea, the greening earth, the shining sky, the gleaming stars I consider great: the majestically approaching thunderstorm, the lightning that shatters houses, the surf-driving storm, the fire-spouting volcano, the earthquake that shakes entire countries I do not consider greater than the previous phenomena, indeed I consider them smaller for they are only effects of much higher laws. . . We want to try to catch sight of the gentle law that guides the human race. . . The law of justice, the law of morals, the law that wants every man to live respected, honored and safe, together with others, so that he can follow his higher human course, acquire the love and admiration of his fellowmen, so that he be protected like a jewel, as every man is a jewel for all other men, this law resides everywhere that men live with other men, and it is shown in man's behavior toward other men. It resides in the love of spouses for one another, in the love of parents for their children, of children for their parents, in the love of brothers and sisters, of friends for one another, in the sweet inclination of the two sexes, in industriousness, whereby we subsist, in our activity for our small circle, far distant places and the whole world. . ." (Adalbert Stifter). So the socialism we are calling for loudly here, and speaking of quietly, is also the gentle reality of the permanent beauty of the life of men together. It is not the wild, ugly transitional destruction of ugly contemporaneity, a destruction which perhaps will have to be a by-product, but which would be ruinous, unsalutary and futile to invoke if the gentle work of the beauty of life had not previously been done in our souls and through them in reality. All innovation has, despite all the ardent enthusiasm that it carries, something desolate, ugly and impious about it. All old things, even the most ill-reputed or archaic institutions such as the military or the national state, because they are old and have a tradition, despite all their decrepitude, needlessness and obsolescence, have a glimmer, as it were, of beauty. Therefore let us be the type of innovators in whose anticipatory imagination, that which they want to create already lives as something finished, tried and tested, and anchored in the past, in primeval and sacred life. Therefore let us destroy mainly by means of the gentle, permanent and binding reality that we build. Our league (*Bund*) is a league of life striving with the eternal powers that link us with the world of reality. Let the idea that drives us be indeed an idea, i.e., a bond that unites us beyond transitory, fragmentary, and superficial temporal phenomena with the calm community of the spirit. This is our socialism, a creating of the future, as if it had existed since all eternity. Let it not come from the excitements and angry, violent reactions of the moment, but from the presence of the spirit, the tradition and heritage of our humanity.

We have digressed in order to express our gratitude to the unions for their struggle for leisure and free time for working people. Let what has been said here be our thanks. As we do not wish to be merely products, results of and reactions to the terrible decaying excrescences of the archaic and obsolete, but rather productive men who lead the sunken spirit, which once was a common spirit and has now become isolation, to new forms and back to life and beauty, our gratitude therefore ought to be productive and point the way to what ought to constitute the leisure and free time of the workers. Only then will a healthy, strong and spiritual people be able to prepare the new reality which must emerge from us as something primeval if it is to be of any use and permanence.

The decrease of working hours creates longer free time for the workers. However much one may rejoice at this fact, one must not ignore what results such achievements have often had: greater exploitation of the workers' strength, increased intensity of work. Often the highly capitalized entrepreneur, e.g., a large stock company, has every reason to rejoice over the workers' victory. All entrepreneurs of a certain sector have, for instance, been forced to shorten working hours, but the large enterprises are often able to compensate for these losses by introducing new machines which chain the worker even more constantly in the service of the high-speed machinery. Thus they gain a great advantage over their medium-sized and smaller competitors. Sometimes, of course, the opposite happens and the huge enterprise is hampered from reshaping its tremendous mechanism, while the medium-sized and small enterpriser, if he has active sales and good credit, can adapt more easily to the new conditions.

Technology almost always has ideas and models on hand to satisfy this need for increased extraction of work out of activities of men who are only servants of the machines.

That is the other, the bitter side of a longer free evening: a more strenuous working day. The living man can, in truth, not only work to live but he wants to feel his life in work, and during work to rejoice in his work. He needs not only recreation, rest and joy in the evening, he needs, above all, pleasure in his activity itself, strong presence of his soul in the functions of his body. Our age has made sport, the unproductive, playful activity of muscles and nerves into a sort of work or profession. In real culture work itself again becomes a playful unwinding of all our energies.

The industrialist will, moreover, in order to regain what the shortening of the working time takes from him, not even have to modify the mechanical apparatus of his enterprise. In the factory there is an additional mechanism not constructed of iron and steel: the work system. A few new regulations, a few new supervisory and foreman positions often speed up an enterprise more than new machines. However, such a system is seldom long-lasting. There is always a silent struggle between the indolence or natural slowness of the worker and the driving energy of the overseers. Over a period of time, when it is a question of man against man, a sort of law of inertia always wins. This fight for slow work has always existed, long before it became a conscious weapon in the class struggle and a form of so-called sabotage. Such sabotage, which calls on the workers, for a certain purpose, to deliver slow, shoddy, bad or even harmful work, can in particular cases, e.g., strikes of postal, railway or dock workers, render excellent services. However it also has its questionable side, since in extreme means of struggle of the workers in their role as producers, it is not always possible to distinguish where the class-conscious militant ends and the irresponsible man begins, spiritually hollow, ruined and degenerate, to whom every form of useful work is abhorrent.

The accelerated work system has only temporary effect, but the machine is relentless. It has its definite number of rounds, its given output, and the worker no longer depends on a more or less human person, but on a metal devil created by men to exploit human energies. The psychological consideration of man's joy in his work plays a subordinate role here; every worker knows and feels with particular bitterness that machines, tools and animals are better treated than working men. This is as far from being a provocative, demogogic exaggeration as anything that has been said above. It is the cold, sober truth. The workers have often been called slaves in a tone of the utmost indignation. However, one should know what one says, and use even a word like "slave" in its sober, literal sense. A slave was a *protégé*, who had to be guided psychologically, for his death cost money: a new slave had to be bought. The terrible thing about the relationship of the modern worker to his master is precisely that he is no such slave, that in most cases the entrepreneur can be completely indifferent as to whether the worker lives or dies. He lives for the capitalist; but he dies for himself. He can be replaced. Machines and horses have to be bought, which involves both procurement costs and secondly, operating costs. So it was with the slave, who first had to be bought and trained even as a child and then provided with subsistence. The modern entrepreneur gets the modern worker free of charge; whether he pays a subsistence wage to one or to the other is indifferent.

Here again in this depersonalization and dehumanization of the relationship between the entrepreneur and the worker, the capitalist system, modern technology and state centralism go hand in hand. The capitalist system itself reduces the worker to a number. Technology, allied with capitalism, makes him a cog in the wheels of the machine. Finally the state sees to it that the capitalist not only has no reason to mourn the worker's death, but even in cases of death or accident has no need to become personally involved with him in any way. The state's insurance institutions can certainly be regarded from many aspects, but this one should not be overlooked. They too replace living humanity by a blindly functioning mechanism.

The limits of technology, as it has been incorporated into capitalism, have gone beyond the bounds of humanity. There is not much concern for the workers' life or health (here one must not think only of the machines; one should also recall the dangerous metal wastes in the polluted air of work-shops and factories, the poisoning of the air over entire cities), and certainly there is no concern for the worker's joy of life or comfort during work.

The Marxists and the masses of workers who are influenced by them are completely unaware of how fundamentally the technology of the socialists differs from capitalist technology in this regard. Technology will, in a cultured people, have to be directed according to the psychology of free people who want to use it. When the workers themselves determine under what conditions they want to work, they will make a compromise between the amount of time they want to spend outside of production and the intensity of work they are willing to accept within production. There will be considerable individual differences; some will work very fast and energetically, so that afterwards they can spend a very long time in rest and recreation, while others will prefer not to degrade any hours of the day to a mere means, and they will want their work itself to be pleasurable and proceed at a comfortable pace. Their slogan will be "Haste makes waste" and their technology will be adapted to their nature.

Today all this does not come into consideration. Technology stands completely under the spell of capitalism. The machine, the tool, man's dead servant has become man's master. Even the capitalist, to a great extent, depends on the mechanism he has introduced, and this is the moment where we can examine the second aspect of the shortened working time. The first was that it served to preserve the worker's strength; we have just seen to what extent the increased intensity of work countervails this tendency. But the shortening of working hours has the further positive effect for the living members of the working class of reducing the number of unemployed.

The industrialist must, namely use his machinery to capacity. In order to be profitable his machines must run for a certain period of time. If his enterprise is to be profitable, he must adjust to his competition at home and abroad, and in many sectors he is compelled to have his machines run day and night so that his power plant pays for itself. Thus when working hours are shortened, he will employ more workers. He will often use the occasion of a struggle with the workers to introduce the 24-hour work period, i.e., a system of alternating shifts. The need for profit, the demands of the system, the workers' demands: all this, conjointly, often leads to the employment of more workers and thus to the decrease in numbers of the so-called industrial reserve army. The limit is always determined by the profitability of the enterprise, whereby a sort of compromise must be made between the requirements of the system and the absorption-capacity of the market.

Often the entrepreneur is forced by his machinery and the number of workers operating these machines to continue running the plant at a certain volume, and if the market can no longer absorb the output, then he must lower prices: for the capitalist market can absorb any articles as long as they are cheap enough. This is the reason why a capitalist often has thousands of employees working day and night and still loses money hour by hour. He accepts this in the hope of better times when prices will rise again. If this hope does not materialize, he will have to shut down a part or all of his plant on certain days.

Our statement that technology presently stands under the spell of capitalism must thus be complemented by the corollary that capitalism, too, in turn is a slave of the technology it has created. This predicament is like that of the magician's apprentice: "The spirits I conjured up, I can't get rid of again!" Whoever has in times of prosperity, of a favorable market adjusted his enterprise at a certain level, no longer has the choice as to how much he must produce. He too is fastened to the wheel of his machines, and often he is crushed together with his workers.

Here we have touched one of the points where capitalist production is most closely linked with speculation. Only a very small man on the scale of capitalism would not be forced into speculation by the conditions of his enterprise and his market. Everyone is a speculator to the extent that his enterprise depends on these two totally unconnected factors: first, the requirements of his apparatus of men and machines, and secondly, the price fluctuations of the world market. Men in this situation who, often for years, pay out a fixed wage week after week to hundreds or thousands of workers while suffering losses week after week, must often exclaim with a moan: "My workers are better off than I!" Often a poor rich man plagued by countless worries can save himself only by successful speculations on the stock-market with a part of his fortune, thus counterbalancing his bad luck in the area of trade speculation, while, on the contrary, one whose business flourishes often can ruin himself by speculations in a completely different field. Whoever is dependent on the capitalist market must speculate, he must accustom himself to speculating in the most varied fields.

The worker who suffers under capitalism knows far too little of this decisive fact. Everyone without exception, suffers immeasurably and has little joy, no real joy, under capitalist conditions. The worker also has too little knowledge of the terrible, degrading and oppressive worries the capitalist faces, the completely unnecessary, and totally unproductive torments and strain he must bear. And the workers are not sufficiently aware of this similarity between themselves and the capitalists. Not only the capitalists, but also many hundreds of thousands in the working force itself draw their profit or their wages from completely useless, unproductive, superfluous work. Precisely today there is a terrible tendency for production to create more and more luxury commodities, including trashy items for the proletariat, and far too few sound and necessary products to meet real needs. The necessary products are becoming more and more expensive, luxury trashier and cheaper—that is the trend.

Let us now return from the digression dedicated to union activities and give a final summary.

We have seen how the entrepreneurs with a stake in capitalism, the manufacturers and merchants, but also the workers with their interest in earning a livelihood, and finally the state, have and continue all to work toward the preservation of the system of capitalist economy. We have further noted how all men are entangled in this mutual exploitation, how all unanimously must protect their special interests and harm the common good, and how all, no matter at what level of capitalism they stand are always threatened by insecurity.

When we saw this, we saw the failure of Marxism, for it claimed that socialism was being prepared in the institutions and catastrophic process of bourgeois society itself, while the struggle of the ever growing, ever more decisive and more revolutionary proletarian masses was a necessity, an historically predestined act to bring about socialism. In reality, however, this struggle of the workers in their role as producers for the capitalist market is only a vicious circle within capitalism. It cannot even be said that this struggle leads to a general improvement of the situation of the working class; all that can be seen is that it and its effects accustom the working class to their situation and to the general conditions of society.

Marxism is one of the factors and not an inessential one, that preserves the capitalist condition, strengthens it and makes its effects on the spirit of the people ever more desolate. The peoples, the bourgeoisie and, equally, the working class are becoming ever more implicated in the conditions of senseless, speculative and cultureless production only for the purpose of acquiring money. In the classes that suffer the most under these conditions, and often live in hardship, deprivation and poverty, clear knowledge, rebellion and the desire for improvement are declining more and more.

Capitalism is not a period of progress, but of decline.

Socialism does not come by the further development of capitalism and cannot be the producers' struggle within capitalism.

These are the conclusions we have reached.

The centuries of which our present one is a part are a time of negation. The associations and corporations, the entire common life of the earlier cultured time, from which we stem, all its beautiful earthly activity and motivation was wrapped in a heavenly illuson. Three things were inseparably united: first, the spirit of unity in life, secondly the symbolic language for an unnamable unity, spirituality and significance of the cosmos as it was truly grasped in the soul of the individual man, and thirdly, superstition.

In our times, the superstitions of the literally-understood Christian dogmatic ideas have come under heavy attack and are being more and more uprooted even among the people. As the stellar universe was being discovered, the earth and man on it became simultaneously smaller and greater. Earthly activity was extended. Fear of devils, heavenly powers, cobolds and demons began to disappear. Man felt more secure in the infinite space of worlds on his circling little star than before on God's grotesque world. Undeniable natural forces whose effects could be precisely measured became known. They could be used and relied on without fear. New methods of work and of processing natural products were discovered. The earth was explored and repopulated over its entire surface; travel and communication go with a speed even we are not yet accustomed to, and which still seems fabulous to us, all round the globe; and in connection with all this the number of people living at the same time has increased enormously. Needs, but also the means of satisfying them have risen tremendously.

By no means has superstition merely been shaken in this our age of negation. Something positive has also replaced it: knowledge of the objective constitution of nature has abolished faith in demonic enemies and friends in nature. Power over nature has followed fear of the sudden whims and treachery of the spirit world, and this death of countless spirits and sprites found its very real expression in the extraordinary rise of the birth-rate of the children of men.

But all deeper feeling, all exuberance and every human unity and bond was deeply interwoven with the spirit-heaven. The stellar worlds we discovered, the natural forces with whose effects we became familiar, are only external; they are useful and they serve external life. Although we express their unity with our interior life in all sorts of ways, sometimes in deep, sometimes in shallow philosophies, theories of nature, and poetic inspirations, it is not a part of us, it has not come to life. Rather, what was alive before, the image, or faith, or ineffable knowledge that the world in its truth, as we bear it in ourselves, is completely different from what the utilitarian senses tell us, and also the genuine community of men in small voluntary groups, related to this world-view—all this declined together with superstition. All advances in science and technology have failed to provide the least substitute for it.

That is why we call these times a period of decline, because the essential trait of culture, the spirit that unites men together has declined.

The attempts to return to the old superstition or to symbolic language that has lost its meaning, these ever renewed efforts of reaction, connected with the weakness and the rootlessness of people addicted to the old patterns, in whom feeling is stronger than reason, are dangerous obstructions, and ultimately also only symptoms of the end. They become even more repugnant when, as easily happens, they are connected with the coercive rule of the state, which is itself organized spiritlessness.

So when we speak of decline, it has nothing in common with the clergy's complaint about the sinfulness of our world or with the call for conversion. This collapse is a transitory epoch, containing in it the seeds for a new beginning, a fresh upturn, a unified culture.

As urgent as it is for us to conceive of socialism, the struggle for new conditions between men as a spiritual movement, i.e., to understand that the only way of arriving at new human relationships is when people moved by the spirit create them for themselves, it is just as important for us to be strong and not to squint backwards towards a past that cannot be brought back. In short, we must not lie to ourselves. The illusion of heaven, truth, philosophy, religion, world view, or whatever one wants to call the attempts to crystalize feeling about the world into words and forms, now exist for us only as individuals. Every attempt to establish communities, sects, churches, associations of any kind on the basis of such spiritual correspondences leads, if not to falsehood and reaction, then at least to mere insubstantial chatter. In everything that goes beyond the world of the senses and of nature, we are deeply lonesome and subject to silent isolation. This means that all our world views contain no overpowering necessity, no ethical cogency, and are not binding on the economy and on society. We must accept this, for it is so, and, since we are living in the age of individualism, we can take it in many ways: gladly or with resignation, despairingly or with desire, indifferently or even rebelliously.

Let us however remember that every delusion, every dogma, every philosophy or religion has its roots not in the external world, but in our inner life. All these symbols, in which men bring nature and the self into harmony, are therefore suited to bringing beauty and justice into the communal life of peoples, because they are reflections of the social drive within us, and because they are our own form itself which has become spirit. All spirit is communal spirit, and there is no individual in whom, awake or asleep, the drive to the whole, to associate with others, to community, to justice, ever rests. The natural compulsion to voluntary association for the purposes of community is inextirpable, but it has been dealt a hard blow and become numbed because for long ages it was connected with the world delusions that had stemmed from it and have now perished or are in the process of decay.

So we do not have to first create a world view for the people; that would be completely artificial, transitory and weak, or even romantic and hypocritical, and today would in fact be subject to fashion. We have the reality of the living, individual communal spirit in us and we must merely let it emerge creatively. The desire to create small groups and communities of justice—not a heavenly delusion or a symbolic form, but earthly social joy and readiness of individuals to form a people—will bring about socialism and the beginning of a real society.

The spirit will act directly, and will create its visible forms out of living flesh and blood: symbols of eternity become communities, incarnations of the spirit become incorporations of earthly justice, the images of the saints in our churches become institutions of the rational economy.

The rational economy: this word is used completely intentionally, for one more thing must be added.

We have called this era a period of decline, because the essential has been weakened and ruined: the common spirit, voluntariness, the beauty of folk-life and its forms. But it cannot be ignored that this time contains much progress. Progress in science, in technology, the unbiased conquest and subjugation of objectified nature is called, by a different word: enlightenment. Reason has become more agile and clear; and as we have won physics—in the widest sense of the term—from nature, and its proves its value by practical application, and as we have, by exploiting the forces of nature, learned to use mathematics, so now, as we apply the technology of human relations on an extraordinarily broad field all round the globe, we will learn to do the right and reasonable thing with frequent application of mathematics, division of labor and scientific methods. Previously industrial technology and economic relationships, both highly developed, were geared to the system of injustice and meaningless power. Both physico-industrial and economico-social technology will now help the new culture, the future people, just as before they served the privileged, the powerful and the stock-market speculators.

Thus, instead of speaking of the period of decline that we are in, we can also, if we wish, speak of progress, in which observation and mastery of nature, technology and rational economics are gaining ever greater ascendancy, until finally the common spirit, voluntariness, and the social drive, which for a few centuries were buried under, will arise again, seize man and bring them together and take control of the new powers.

Once the same trend of the spirit in individuals has taken hold of these new capacities with its natural compulsion and joined them in solid groups, the idea, the holistic perspective, which transforms individual, separate phenomena into coherent unities, will emerge again from the spirit of individual men and become a league of men, a corporate body and a binding form. Once this earthly-corporeal form of the spirit is there, then it could easily happen that again men will have centuries of spiritual exuberance, of cogent world-view or delusion. We do not seek to be thus overwhelmed, we guard against it and are not avid for allegiance. We too know far too little of the trajectories of human history to be able to say with any probability that this circle must again be closed and that again idea and union would have to be linked with the cosmic-religious, artificial form of superstition, and that at a further stage, together with superstition, the common spirit would be broken again and isolation restored, and so on. We have no right to make such constructions. It may be that this all is a necessity, but the future may be completely different. We are still far from such knowledge. Our task now stands clearly before us: not falsehood, but truth. Not the artificiality of an imitation of religion, but the *reality of social creation without restricting complete spiritual independence and multiplicity of individuals.*

The new society we want to prepare, whose cornerstone we are about to lay, will not be a return to any old structures. It will be the old in a new form, a culture with the means discovered by civilization in these recent centuries.

This new people, however, does not come by itself: it "must" not come at all, as the false science of the Marxist understands this "must." It *should* come, because we socialists *want* it, and because we already carry the model of such a people in our spirits.

How will we start? How will socialism come? What should be done? Done first? Done right away? To answer this will be our final task.

6.

It was a memorable moment in the history of our era, when Pierre Joseph Proudhon, after the French February revolution of the year 1848, told his people what it had to do to establish a society of justice and freedom. He was still living, like all his revolutionary compatroits of the time, completely in the tradition of the revolution which had erupted externally in 1789 and had, as was then felt, been nipped in the bud by the counterrevolution and subsequent governments. He said: The revolution put an end to feudalism. Something new must replace it. Feudalism was an order in the area of the economy of the state, it was an articulated, military system of dependencies. For centuries it had been undermined by freedoms; civil liberties had gained more and more ground. However, they also destroyed the old order and security, the old associations and leagues. A few men became rich under the new freedom and mobility, while the masses were exposed to hardship and insecurity. How can we both preserve, extend and create freedom for all, as well as bring about security, the great equalization of property and conditions of life, the new order?

The revolutionaries, he says, do not yet know that the revolution will put an end to militarism, i.e., to the government; that its task is to replace politics by social life, political centralism by a direct unity of economic interests, an economic center which does not rule over persons, but takes care of business.

You Frenchmen, he says, are small and medium-sized farmers, small and medium-sized craftsmen; you are active in agriculture, industry, transportation and communications. Until now you needed kings and their officials in order to come together and protect yourselves one from the other. In 1793 you abolished the king of the state, but you retained the king of the economy, gold. Because you thus left misfortune, disorder and insecurity in the country, you had to let the kings and officials and armies return. Do away with the authoritarian intermediaries. Abolish the parasites. See to the direct unity of your interests. Then you will have society as the heir to feudalism and the state.

What is gold? What is capital? It is not a thing like a shoe or a table or a house. It is not a thing, it is nothing real. Gold is the sign for a relationship. Capital is something that goes back and forth as a relationship between men. It is something between men. Capital is credit, credit is mutuality of interests. You are now in the revolution. The revolution—enthusiasm, a spirit of trust, the exuberance of equalization, the desire to go for the whole—has come over you, has arisen among you: create for yourselves direct mutuality. Set up an institution whereby you come to one another with the production of your work without any parasitic, vampire-like intermediaries. Then you will need no tutelary authority, nor the transfer of the absolute power of the political government to economic life, of which the newest bunglers, the Communists, speak. The task is: to assert and create freedom in the economy and public life and to see to an equalization to abolish hardship, insecurity, and property, which is not the ownership of things but the domination of men and slave-ownership, and interest, which is usury. Create an exchange bank!

What is an exchange bank? Nothing but the external form, the objective institution for freedom and equality. Whoever is engaged in useful work—the farmer, the craftsman, the workers association—should all simply continue to work. Work need not be organized, i.e., commanded by the authorities, or nationalized. Cabinetmaker, make furniture; shoemaker, make boots; baker, bake bread; and so on, in the production of everything the people needs. Cabinetmaker, you have no bread? Of course you cannot go to the baker and offer him chairs and cabinets he does not need. Go to the exchange bank and have your orders and your products be changed into universally valid checks. Proletarians, you want no longer to go to the entrepreneur in order to work for wages? You want to be independent? But you have no work-shop, no tools, no food? You cannot wait and you must hire yourself out right away? But don't you have customers? Don't the other proletarians, don't you proletarians, one and all, prefer to purchase your products from one another, without intermediary of the exploitatory middle-men? Then see to your own purchases and sales, you dolts! The clientele is valid. The clientele is money, as that is called today. Must the sequence always be: poverty—slavery—work—product? Mutuality changes the course of things. Mutuality restores the order of nature. Mutuality abolishes the rule of money. Mutuality is primary: the spirit between men that allows all men who want to work to do so and to satisfy their needs.

Seek no guilty ones, he says, all are guilty. Some enslave, and others take away the most basic necessities or leave only the barest necessity, or serve the enslaving lords as agents and supervisers. Not from the spirit of revenge, anger or destructiveness will the new be created. Destruction must be done out of a constructive spirit. Revolution and conservation are not mutually exclusive.

Stop copying the ancient Romans. The Jacobite dictatorship played its role in the past, but the great theater of the tribunes and the beautiful gesture does not create your society. It must be carried out in reality. You make useful objects in sufficient quantity; you would like to consume useful things in just distribution; so you must exchange correctly.

There is no value, he says, that is not created by work; the workers have created the superiority of the capitalists, and you have not been able to keep and use the values you create because you are isolated and propertyless men who increase the wealth of the owners and thereby provide them with power over slaves and property. But how childish it is, he could say, therefore only to stare at the present stockpile of accumulated property in the hands of the privileged and to think only of taking it away from them by political or violent methods. It is always in flux, always in circulation. Today it flows from the capitalist via the workers as consumers back to the capitalist; set up new institutions by transforming your mutual behavior so that it will go from the capitalist to the consuming workers, but from them not back to the capitalists, but into the hands of the same workers, the producing workers.

With incomparable power, with a great combination of sobriety and warmth, of passion and objectivity, Proudhon said this to his people. In the moment of revolution, dissolution, transition and the possibility of comprehensive and fundamental measures, he proposed the individual steps and decrees that would have created the new society and would have been the last act of the government, and m\de that government really what it was called: a provisional governmₑnt.

The voice was there, but the listeners were missing. The right time was there but it passed, and now it is gone forever.

Proudhon the man knew what we socialists have re-discovered: socialism is possible at all times and impossible at all times. It is possible when the right men are there who want it, i.e., who carry it into action, and it is impossible when men do not want it or only supposedly want it but cannot act accordingly. So this man was not heard. Men heard instead another voice which presented the false science we have examined and rejected, which taught that socialism is the crowning of the capitalist big industry; that it comes only when very few capitalists have private ownership of institutions that have already almost become socialist so that it would be easy for the united proletarian masses to transfer it from private ownership to social ownership.

Instead of Pierre Joseph Proudhon, the man of synthesis, Karl

Marx, the man of analysis, was heard and so the dissolution, decay and decline was allowed to continue.

Marx, the man of analysis, worked with fixed, rigid concepts imprisoned in their word-casings. With these concepts he wanted to express and almost dictate the laws of development.

Proudhon, the man of synthesis, taught us that the closed conceptual words are only symbols for incessant movement. He dissolved concepts in streaming continuity.

Marx, the man of apparently strict science, was the legislator and dictator of development. He made pronouncements on it; and as he determined it, so it should be once and for all. Events were to behave like a finished, closed, dead reality. Therefore Marxism exists as a doctrine and almost a dogma.

Proudhon, who sought to solve no problem with the thing-words, who instead of closed things posited movements, and relations, instead of apparent being, becoming, instead of crude visibility, an invisible fluctuation, who finally — in his most mature writings — transformed the social economy into psychology, while transforming psychology from rigid individual psychology, which makes an isolated thing out of individual man, into social psychology, which conceives of man as a member of an infinite, inseparable and inexpressible stream of becoming. So there is no Proudhonism, but only a Proudhon. So what Proudhon said of truth for a certain moment can no longer apply today, when things have been allowed to continue for decades. Valid is only what is eternal in Proudhon's ideas; no attempt should be made to return slavishly to him, or to any past historical moment.

What the Marxists have said of Proudhon, that his socialism is a socialism of the petit-bourgeois and small farmers, is, let us repeat it, completely true and is his highest title to fame. His socialism, in other words, of the years 1848 to 1851 was the socialism of the French people in the years 1848 to 1851. It was the socialism that was possible and necessary at that moment. Proudhon was not a Utopian and a prophet; not a Fourier and not a Marx. He was a man of action and realization.

We are speaking here expressly of Proudhon, the man of 1848 to 1851. This man said, and the age was constituted for him to say: "You revolutionaries, if you do that, you will achieve the great transformation."

The man of later years, from whom we have as much to learn as from the one of 1848, did not like to repeat the revolutionary words he had spoken after the revolution, in a vain melodramatic or pornographic self-imitation. Everything has its time, and every time after the revolution is a time before the revolution for all whose life did not stop at the great moment of the past. Proudhon lived on, though he bled from many wounds. He now asked himself: "I said, if you do it; but why didn't they do it?" He found the answer and he wrote it down in his later works, the answer that in our language is: because the spirit was missing.

It was missing then and it has been missing for sixty years and has been lost and sunken ever deeper. Everything we have shown till now can be summed up in one sentence: waiting for the supposed right moment foreseen in history has postponed this goal further and further and pushed it into blurred darkness; trust in progress and development was the name of regression and this "development" adapted the external and internal conditions more and more to degradation and made the great change ever more remote. The Marxists will be right with their "It is not yet time!" as long as men believe them, and they will never be less, but always more right. Is it not the most frightful madness that ever lived and happened, that a saying is true, *because* it was spoken and heard credulously? And must not everyone notice that the attempt to express becoming as if it were final, completed being, if it wins power over the minds of men, must ultimately cripple the powers of form and creativity?

That is the reason for our untiring attack on Marxism. That is why we almost cannot let it go and must hate it with all our heart. It is not a description and a science, which it pretends to be, but a negating, destructive and crippling appeal to impotence, lack of will, surrender and indifference. Social Democracy's bee-like work on details — incidentally Social Democracy is not Marxism — is only the other side of this impotence and only expresses that socialism is not there: for socialism in small and great matters aims for the whole. Not detailed work as such is to be rejected, but only how it is practiced, driven about in the circle of existing nonsense like a dry leaf in a tornado.

The so-called revisionists, who are especially zealous about details and whose critique of Marxism often coincides with ours — no wonder, they have taken it in great part from anarchists, from Eugen Dühring and other independent socialists — have gradually fallen in love with something that could be called tactics of principle, so that together with Marxism they have also rejected socialism almost down to the last trace. They are in the process of founding a party to promote the working class in capitalist society by parliamentary and economic means. The Marxists believe in progress à la Hegel, while the revisionists are adherents of evolution à la Darwin. They no longer believe in catastrophe and suddenness; capitalism will not become socialism by a sudden revolution, they believe, but it will gradually assume a more tolerable form.

A few of them would prefer to admit that they are not socialists, and go surprisingly far in their adaptation to parliamentarism and party politics, vote-getting and monarchism. Others still consider themselves completely to be socialists. They believe they see a constant, slow, but unhalting improvement of the private situation of the workers, of the workers' share in production by so-called industrial constitutionalism, and of public and legal conditions through the expansion of democratic institutions in all countries. From the failure of Marxist doctrine, which they both recognize and partially cause, they draw the conclusion that capitalism is already well on the way to socialism and that the energetic promotion of this development is the mission of socialists. With this view they are not so very far from what Marxism said from the first, and the so-called radicals were always on the same path and have only the wish that this view not be told to the masses of voters who have been whipped up to and held together by revolutionarism.

The true relation of the Marxists to the revisionists is as follows: Marx and the best of his disciples had in mind the whole of our conditions in their historical context and tried to arrange the details of our social life under general concepts. The revisionists are epigonal skeptics who see clearly that the established generalities do not coincide with the newly arisen realities, but who still have the need for a new and essentially different total understanding of our time.

Marxism had for a time led great numbers of the disinherited to awareness of their poverty, dissatisfaction and an idealistic mood favorable to an overall change. That could not last, because under the influence of this scientific folly the masses shifted to waiting and became incapable of any socialist activity. So gradually dullness and calm would have long since returned to the masses, if they had not been constantly spurred on by political and demagogical methods. The revisionists now see that the very worst barbarities of early capitalism have been removed, that the workers have grown more accustomed to proletarian conditions and that capitalism by no means is nearing its fall. In all this, of course, we see the tremendous danger of the continuation of capitalism. In truth the situation of the working class — as seen as a whole — has not improved. On the contrary, life has become more difficult and unpleasant. It has become so unpleasant that the workers have become joyless, hopeless and impoverished in spirit and character. Above all, however, the struggle for socialism, the right struggle, does not hinge exclusively on feelings of pity or primarily on the fate of a certain class of men. It has to do with a complete transformation of the foundations of society. Its goal is a new creation.

Our workers have lost this mood (for it was never more than a mood) more and more, because in Marxism the elements of dissolution and impotence were from the first stronger than the forces of indignation, and lacked every positive content. The phenomenon of revisionism and its indulgent skepticism is only the "ideological superstructure" over the inaction, indecision, and complacency of the masses and shows, to all who already knew it, that the working force is not the chosen people of God, of development by historical necessity, but rather the part of the people suffering most severely, and because of psychic changes that accompany misery it will find it hardest to acquire knowledge. It is best to avoid all generalizations in this area. The working class is highly disparate, and suffering has always had very different effects on very different men. But a major part of suffering is the realization of one's bad situation; and how many proletarians to this extent undergo not the least suffering!

We know how the relations have changed in these times after the revolution failed, in these sixty years before the revolution. These were the decades of adaptation of capitalism, of adaptation to proletarization, and it is truly an adaptation that in many ways has already become hereditary. There is a deterioration of the relations between men, which has already noticeably become a decay of very many bodies of individual men.

That is a tremendous danger we are speaking of here. We have said: socialism does not have to come, as the Marxists think. Now we say: the moment can come, if the various peoples continue to hesitate, the time will come when socialism will no longer abe possible for them. Men may yet act so foolishly, so basely toward one another. They may surrender so utterly to enslavement and accept their own brutality: all that is something between men, something functional and can be changed in the next generation or already for men now living, if a dicisive, vibrant emotion serves them. As long as it is a question of these social or, as they are usually called, psychological relations, the situation is not yet bad. Mass misery, poverty, hunger, homelessness, psychological demoralization and depravity, as well as pleasure-seeking, stupid luxury, militarism, spiritlessness — all this, bad as it is, can be cured if the right doctor comes: out of the creative spirit, the great revolution and regeneration. However, if all the hardship and pressure and, unspirit ceases to be something between men, a disturbance of their relationships that resides in the soul, if it is no longer a disturbance in the complex of relations between men, which we call soul, if instead chronic undernourishment, alcoholism, long-lasting brutalization, continuous dissatisfaction, acute spiritlessness, with far-reaching effects result in changes of the individual bodies, whose significance to the soul and to the social structure is as the spider to its web, then no remedy can help any more and it may happen that entire sections of the people or entire peoples are damned to destruction. They perish as peoples have always perished: other, healthy peoples become their masters and a mixture of peoples, and sometimes even partial extermination takes place — if, at least, other, healthy peoples still exist. One should not play facile games with analogies from earlier periods of the history of nations. For when the time comes, things need not again proceed as they did in the times of the so-called migration of nations. We are living in times of the beginning of mankind, and it cannot be completely ruled out that this incipient mankind might be the beginning of the end of mankind. Perhaps no age has ever seen the end of the world looming so dangerously before its eyes, as our does.

Mankind, in the sense of a real complex of relations, a world society held together by external bonds and an inner attraction and urge surpassing national bounds, of course does not yet exist. Surrogates for it are, however, there, and they may be more than an *ersatz*. They could be the beginning: the world market, international treaties or governmental policies, international organizations and congresses of the most manifold types, traffic and communications around the globe, all this creates more and more, if not equality, then at least an assimilation of interests, customs, art or its modish substitute, the spirit of technology, the political forms. Workers are also being lent more and more from some nations to others. Furthermore all spiritual reality—religion, art, language, common spirit in general—is doubly there or seems to us duplicated by a natural compulsion: first, in the individual soul as a quality or faculty, and secondly, outside, as something interwoven between men and creating organizations and associations. All this is expressed imprecisely. What can be corrected in passing will be done immediately, but we cannot at this time descend to the very bottom of these abysses of language criticism and theory of ideas (the two things belong together). All this is merely mentioned in order to say: *humanitas, humanité*, humanity and mankind—for which we now say, with an expression of false pitying condescension, weakened and deprived of depth, "humaneness"—all these words originally referred only to the mankind living and ruling in the individual. It was once very strongly present, very physically felt, at least in the high times of Christianity. We will arrive at a real humanity in the external sense only when reciprocity as identical community has come for the humanity concentrated in the individual and the humanity growing between the individuals. The plant dwells in the seed, just as the seed is only the quintessence of the infinite chain of ancestral plants. Mankind obtains its genuine existence from the humanness of the individual, just as this humanness of the individual is only the heir of the infinite generations of the past and all their mutual relationships. What has become is the becoming, the microcosm is the macrocosm. The individual is the people, the spirit is the community, the idea is the bond of unity.

But for the first time in the history of the few thousand years that we know, mankind wants to become externally unified in the complete sense and scope. The earth has been almost completely explored, soon it will be almost completely inhabited and owned. What is needed now is renewal such as never existed before in the world of men we know. That is the decisive trait of our time, this new thing that ought to overwhelm us far more. Mankind all around the globe wants to be created, and wants this at a moment when a mighty renewal must come over mankind, if the beginning of a unified mankind is not to be its end. Formerly such renewal was often identical with the new peoples that emerged from rest and cultural mixture, or with new countries into which migrations took place. The more similar the peoples become to one another, the more densely countries are inhabited, the less hope there is for such renewal from the outside or from within. Those who already want to despair of our own peoples or at least believe that the external impulse for the radical renewal of minds and vital energy must come from the outside, from old peoples who have recently awakened from a healing sleep, can still build some hopes on the Chinese, Indian or maybe the Russian peoples. Some can still hope that behind the puerile North American barbarity there still slumbers perhaps a still hidden idealism and surplus energy of ardent spirit that could erupt marvellously. However, it is conceivable that we who are 40 or 50 years old will yet experience the disappointment of these romantic expectations, and that the Chinese will follow the Japanese in imitating the West, that the Indians will arise, only to quickly glide into the channels of decay, etc. Assimilation is proceeding very rapidly. Civilization is spreading, and with it a veritable physical and physiological decadence.

We must plunge into this abyss in order to obtain the courage and urgency that we need. This time the renewal must be greater and different than it was in any known times. We are not seeking only the culture and human beauty of life together. We are seeking a remedy; we are seeking salvation. The greatest exterior that ever existed on earth must be created and is already being prepared in privileged strata: global mankind. Yet is cannot come through external bonds, through treaties and a governmental structure or a world state of horrid invention, but only by way of the most individual individualism and the re-establishment of the smallest groups: of the communities, above all. A comprehensive society must be built, and the construction must begin on a small scale; we must extend ourselves into all latitudes and we can do it only if we dig very deep, for no help can come any more from the outside. No more unoccupied land invites the densely crowded peoples to settle; we must establish mankind and can find it only in humanness. We can let it arise only out of the voluntary bond of individuals and out of the community of originally independent men who are naturally drawn to one another.

Only now can we socialists breathe freely and accept the inescapable hardship, our task, as a piece of our existence. Now we feel the living certainty that our idea is not an opinion which we adopt but a mighty compulsion that places us before the choice: either to experience the real destruction of mankind in advance and to watch its beginnings eroding around us, or to make the first beginning of the ascent with our own action.

The end of the world, which we here allow to threaten as a spectre of possible reality, of course does not mean sudden extinction. We warn against the analogy and inclination to find an inviolable sort of rule in it, because we know of a few times of decline which were then followed by great periods. When we visualize with what unparalleled speed the nations and their classes are becoming more alike in this capitalist civilization: how the proletarians are becoming dull, submissive, crude, external, and to an increasing extent, alcoholics, how together with their loss of religion they are beginning to lose every sort of internal feeling and responsibility, how all this is beginning to take physical effect; how the upper classes are losing the power for politics, for a comprehensive view and decisive action, how art is being replaced by foppery, modish frippery, and archeological or historical imitation, how with the old religion and morality every firm standard, every sacred allegiance, every firmness of character is being lost, how women are being drawn into the whirlpool of superficial sensuality, of colorful, decorative lasciviousness; how the natural unreflected population increase is beginning to decline in all strata of the people and being replaced by sex without children under the guidance of science and technology; how irresponsibility is pervading precisely the better elements among the proletarians and citizens, who can no longer bear to do joyless work under the prevailing conditions. If we see how all this is beginning to turn into neurosis and hysteria in all strata of society, then one must ask where the people is that will pull itself together for recovery, for the creation of new institutions? Is it quite certain, are there unmistakable signs that we will rise again, as formerly a new beginning came out of decaying refined civilization and fresh blood? Is it certain that mankind is not a temporary, inaccurate word for what will later be: the end of nations? Already the voices of degenerate, unrestrained and uprooted females and their male consorts are proclaiming promiscuity and seeking to replace the family with the pleasure of variety, free, unrestrained union, fatherhood with state motherhood insurance. The spirit needs freedom and contains it. Where spirit creates such unions as family, cooperative, professional group, community and nation, there is freedom and mankind too can come about. But do we know, can we be sure that we can endure what now is beginning to rage instead of the spirit missing in the coercive institutions of domination that have replaced it: freedom without spirit, sensual freedom, freedom to irresponsible pleasure? or whether the inevitable result of all this will not be the most gruesome torments and desolation, the most decrepit weakness and dull apathy? Whether a moment of ardent emotion, of rebirth, of the great period of the federation of cultural communities will ever come to us? Times when song dwells over the people, when towers bear the unity and enthusiasm to heaven and great works are created to represent the people's greatness by towering men in whose spirit the people is concentrated?

We do not know, and *therefore* we know that the attempt is our task. Every alleged science of the future has now been swept away completely. Not only do we know no laws of development. We even know the mighty danger that we may be too late already, that all our attempts and actions may perhaps no longer help. And so we have cast off the last bonds from us, in all our knowledge, we know nothing more. We stand like primitive men before something undescribed and indescribable. We have nothing before us and everything only in us: in us the reality or efficacy not of future mankind, but of past mankind which therefore exists essentially in us. The accomplishment is in us. The undeceivable duty that sends us on our way is in us. The image of what fulfillment should become is in us. The need to leave baseness and misery behind is in us. Justice that is without doubt and relentless is in us. Decency that seeks mutual response is in us, and reason that recognizes the interests of all.

Those who feel as is here written, whose greatest courage grows out of the greatest need, who wish to attempt the renewal despite everything—let them gather around now; they are the ones being called; let them tell the nations what must be done, and show the peoples how to begin.

7.

Times have become different from what Proudhon described in 1848. Dispossession has increased in every way. We have moved further from socialism than sixty years ago.

Sixty years ago Proudhon could in a moment of revolution, of desire to reshape the whole, say to his people what had to be done at that moment.

Today, even if the people should rise up, the point which then was so important is no longer alone decisive. Also in two respects there is no longer a complete people: what is called the proletariat will never by itself be the embodiment of a people, while the nations are so dependent on one another in production and trade that a single people no longer is a people. But mankind is far from being a unity, and will never be until new small units, communities and peoples have again come into being.

Proudhon was completely right, especially at that moment of the elevation of spiritual and psychic life, of communal life, as well as the originality and decisiveness of individuals that accompanies every revolution, and in the particular circumstances of France at that time, which though it was markedly a land of monetary and share-holding capitalism, still was not a land of capitalist big industry and large land-owners. He was right to regard the circulation and abolition of enrichment by interest as the cornerstone of every reform and the point where a start could be made most speedily, thoroughly and painlessly.

Our conditions truly have three points where unjustified enrichment, exploitation, men working not for themselves but for others arise. This type of constant source and permanent cause is what matters everywhere in the movement of the social processes, just as in movements in physics, chemistry or astronomy. It is always wrong and unproductive to inquire about a unique cause in any past or primeval condition: nothing can come about only once, everything is in constant becoming, and there are no original things, only constant movements and constant relations.

The three cardinal points of economic slavery are the following:

First, private ownership of the land. It results in the supplicant, dependent attitude of the unpropertied person, who wants to live, toward the one who deprives him of the possibility to till the soil and to use the products of the soil directly or indirectly. Out of private ownership of the land and its corollary, non-ownership, there arise slavery, subservience, tribute, rent, interest, the proletariat.

Secondly, the circulation of goods in an exchange economy by means of a vehicle of exchange that serves every need non-expirably and unchangeably. A golden gem, though it remain unchanged for centuries, has value only for the person who esteems owning it so highly for the satisfaction of his need for jewelry or vanity that he is willing to give up products of his labor to own it. Most goods also lose materially in value through lying inert or through use and they are quickly destroyed in consumption. They are produced for the purpose of exchange, to obtain objects of use in return, which were produced for the same purpose. Money is a fateful exception, for it is exchanged but not truly used. Statements by monetary theorists to the contrary reflect a bad conscience. If therefore in a just exchange economy, where a product is supposed to be exchanged for one of equal value, a medium of circulation will be necessary corresponding to our money and probably called "money." However it will not have a decisive quality of our money: the quality of having absolute value and also of serving people who have not earned it, to the detriment of others. It is not the possibility of theft which is to be excluded here; theft of any type of money can occur just as of any other goods, and moreover theft is also a sort of work, in fact a very exhausting and on the whole rather unprofitable one and not very enjoyable in a good society. The intention here is, rather, to point out that the harmfulness of modern money lies not only in its interest-bearing value but also in its non-consumability and permanency and its non-disappearance in consumption. The idea that money would be made harmless if it became a mere work-slip and no longer a commodity, is completely false and could make sense only for state slavery where free trade would be replaced by dependence on bureaucratic authority, determining how much each had to work and consume. But in a free exchange economy money must, on the contrary, become like all other commodities, from which it differs essentially today and still remain a general means of exchange: it must, like every commodity, have the double character of exchange and consumption. The possibility, even in a society of just exchange, if the means for exchange is non-consumable and does not lose its value with time, of attaining harmful ownership of a great amount and thereby achieving tributary rights, cannot be denied offhand, although in known history, inheritances and the like played only a subordinate role compared with power and state protection in the origin of big land ownership and consequently in every type of exploitation. Therefore Silvio Gesell's suggestion is valuable, namely to find a form of money that does not, like today, gain value with the years, but on the contrary from the beginning progressively loses value, so that the person who obtains a piece of currency in exchange for his commodity will have no more pressing interest than to exchange it again for a product as soon as possible, etc. Silvio Gesell is one of the very few who have learned from Proudhon, recognized his greatness, and, based on him, arrived at further ideas independently. His description of how this new money brings lively movement into the flow of circulation, how each one can have no other interest in production and in obtaining the means of exchange except consumption, sprang completely from the spirit of Proudhon who taught how the rapid monetary circulation would introduce joy and vitality into private and public life, while a stoppage in the market and the slow circulation of permanent money also cause our energies to stop and our soul to stagnate. Here it is not a question of the future, whether an objective means of exchange can be found that does not contain the danger of plundering — a question for which the important thing is that it is asked at all — but whether the money-circulation is or may have been the point-of-departure to affect the other two points decisively. Here it must, however, be said that if at a certain point in history, as was the case in 1848 in France, mutuality had been introduced into the exchange economy, it would have marked the end of big land-ownership and surplus value.

The third key feature of economic slavery is, accordingly, surplus value. The first thing that must be said is that a lot of mischief can be played with the concept of value, if one does not explain clearly what one means by it and then hold strictly to one's definition. Value contains a demand in its meaning; the meaning become clear when one thinks that the answer of the potential purchaser follows upon the naming of the price: the item is not worth that much. Value thus first seeks to avoid arbitrariness. We narrow down the concept still further when we see it in the sense of the right value, the true value. Value is what the price should be, but is not. This relationship is contained in the price-relationship of every commodity. In this meaning the word "value" contains, as everyone notices who pays attention to its use, the ideal, or social, demand that the price be equal to the value, or in other words, that the total sum of all real work-wages be equal to the total sum of the prices for the final states of the commodities. Since, of course, men who stand in opposition as individuals, exploit for profit every advantage, not only that of property, also that of the rareness of the desired products, of demand increased by special causes, of the consumer's ignorance, etc., in reality the sum of the named price is much, much higher than the sum of the wages. While the workers in certain categories also enjoy a part of these particular advantages under some circumstances in the form of higher "wages," which in comparison with the wages of their brothers engaged in equally strenuous work is not only wages, but also profit, no detail of the complex economic life can change anything about the fact that work cannot with its wage buy everything that it produces. Instead a considerable part is left over for the purchasing power of profit. As was suggested above, the intermediary stages of production, which already enter the market as commodities, have been left out of consideration here for, if one looks into the matter closely, they are bought neither with wages nor with profit from one capitalist producer by another, but with capital, i.e., as we will soon see in more detail, with something that has sneaked into the place of credit or mutuality. Of course, work is ultimately what must supply the interest for this capital. It is hidden in the prices and was already named above in another form as profit resulting from ownership; for capital is the form of circulation of land-ownership that has been made fluid and mobile and of its products achieved through labor. Even for those who in appearance are not owners of land, it is the means of advancing wages to labor for a product that is still in the process of becoming or of remitting wages to labor during the transition of a product from one state of processing to the other or acquiring products by trading and keeping them in storage. Soon we will deal with these different forms of capital and with the distinction of capital into thing-reality, genuine reality of the spirit, and false capital.

What we call value thus arises only through work to improve the ground and to extract and further process the products of the earth. But if the workers are compelled to hire themselves out, to surrender the results of their work-achievement to others for commercial use, in return for a certain compensation, a disproportion arises between the value of the products they have produced and the price of the products they can buy for their own use. The precise point at which they are robbed can be disregarded here, whether in the payment to them — their wage is too low — or in their purchases — the commodities are too expensive. The main thing is not to think of absolute quantities, but of a relation, which in this case is disproportionate and to remember that all profit of the capitalists arises from the discount which they force the workers to accept, no matter at what point, from the proceeds of their work, because of their difficult situations, i.e., that the discount from the workers' wages or their lessened value is equal to the capitalists' profit or surplus value. Here too it is not examined at what point profit flows to the capitalists, nor is a closer investigation made as to whether this question is not falsely posed since again it attempts to place an absolute instead of a correlation, it is only pointed out that profit is distributed at various rates to land-owners, money-capitalists, entrepreneurs, merchants and all their helpers, officials, "mental" workers, and others occupying a privileged position in capitalism. And moreover it must be stressed that it is a question of constructions, which however are completely necessary: not the whole income of persons who have a part in capitalism is profit, they too accomplish work. And not everything that "workers" consume is wages for labor; they too, though often at very slight rates, participate in the profit economy. It would be going too far to divide work into productive and unproductive work; and—which is not the same—separating the produced goods into necessary and luxury commodities. Here it must merely be pointed out in this context that very many people privileged within capitalism not only perform some work but no doubt also productive work, just as on the other hand the workers too perform much completely or partly unproductive work. Secondly, not only necessary but also luxury goods enter into the workers' consumption. All these details, which are of great significance for the real life of our time, could be mentioned here. Here it is a question of pointing out that the one-sided emphasis on the wage-question by the workers and their unions is related to the false conception of surplus value by the Marxists. We have seen above how wage and price are interconnected; we have now pointed out that the view that the so-called surplus value is an absolute quantity that arises from enterprise and flows from there into the other categories of capital is completely false. Surplus value, like wage or price, is a relation and arises in the entire flow of the economic process, not at a particular spot. Marxism's whole fateful focus on enterprise, especially on industrial enterprise arises from the error under discussion here. In this they believe they have discovered the Archimedic point of capitalism. The truth is simply that each and every profit is subtracted from work, or in other words: that there is no productivity of property and no productivity of capital but only a productivity of work. Knowledge of this is indeed a basic point of knowledge of socialism and only because of this knowledge, which they share with all other socialists—Proudhon gave it classical expression in his splendid polemics with Bastiat and in many other places—only therefore can the Marxists call themselves socialists, in the broadest sense of the word. They too know this: the profitability of property and of capital are only a deceitful form for something that is in reality robbery against the productivity of labor. From this basic knowledge, however, the Marxists in their theory and the syndicalists in their practice have drawn conclusions of the most audacious falsity. The Marxists believed that because they had a cause, they had a primary, absolute cause. Work, the working conditions, and the process of production were for them from then on the last work, that explained everything; hence the grotesque wrongness of their materialist conception of history, their laws of development, their expectation of constant concentration and of the great crisis and collapse, etc. They would only have had to investigate further, and ever further—from where then does the workers' hardship come?—and they would have come upon land ownership and the unexpirability and unconsumability of money, and then the state, and the spirit and its ups and downs, and they would have found that the conditions including the state and capital and private property, exist in our attitude and that ultimately everything depended on the relationship of individuals and their energy to the institutions, which as rigid relics of energy and usually of the impotence of individuals of former generations weigh down as a heavy burden on a time. Depending on the point of view and the imagery, one can call the economic conditions, the political relations, religion, etc. as a whole, either the burdensome superstructure, or the basis of life for the individuals of a time; but never can the view be anything but wrong if it regards the economic or social "conditions" as the "material" foundation of a time, and the spirit and its forms as only the "ideological superstructure" or duplication and mirror-image. Of such significance as the knowledge of surplus value was, i.e., the exposé of private property and money-capital as the plunderer of labor, so ruinous was the false belief that the point had been discovered where surplus value "originates." Surplus value resides in circulation; it originates in the purchase of a commodity as much and as little as in the paying of a worker. Expressed in yet another way—since we can speak only in images, truth must be encircled with attempts at description from various standpoints, and we must make all the more use of this approach, the more complicated and fragmentated are the phenomena that we wish to capture in our comprehensive generalities— : the cause of surplus value is not work, but the hardship of the workers. The hardship of the working people lies, as said above, outside the production process, and all the more so the cause of this hardship, and so on, in the circulation of the entire profit and land ownership economy and then out of these encrustations into their causes, the character of the people who move in them and are moved or let themselves be hindered in their movements by them, and then from these back to the men of former generations. Not the capitalist production-process is the ultimate cause of the origin of surplus value; scholars who need an ultimate cause for human relations should note once and for all that Adam is the next-to-the-last and the very last and wonderfully beautiful absolute is God himself. And even he has become unfaithful to his absolutism, for six whole days, since a real absolutist would consider himself far too good for work. He would sit on his throne, i.e., on himself, and say to himself and by himself: I am the world!

The capitalist production process is a key point for the emancipation of work only in a negative respect. It does not lead to socialism by its own further development and immanent laws; not through the workers' struggle in their role as producers can it be transformed decisively in favor of labor, but only if the workers stop playing their role as capitalist producers. Whatever any man, even the worker, does within the structure of capitalism, everything draws him only deeper and deeper into capitalist entanglement. In this role the workers too are participants in capitalism, though their interests are not self-selected but are indoctrinated into them by the capitalists and though in every essential they reap not the advantages but the disadvantages of the injustice into which they are placed. Liberation is possible only for those who can step out of capitalism mentally and physically, who cease playing a role in it and begin to be men. One begins to be a man by no longer working for the non-genuine, profit and its market, and by restoring the submerged true relation between need and work, between hunger and the hands. What must be done is to draw the right conclusion from the basic socialist insight: only work creates values, and that conclusion is: away from the interest market! The work market and its spirit, the relationship between work and consumption and the reason for work, still has to be established.

Today the call for socialism is going to all, not in the belief that all could or would answer it, but with the wish to help some to an awareness that they belong together in the league of beginners.

The men who can and will no longer bear it, those are the ones being called here. To the masses, the peoples of mankind, rulers and subjects, heirs and the disinherited, privileged and cheated, must be said: it is a titanic, inextinguishable shame of the times that the economy is run for profit instead of to fill the needs of men united in communities. All your militarism, your system of state, all your repression of freedom, all your class hatred comes from the brutal stupidity that rules over you. *If suddenly the great moment of revolution came to you peoples, one and all, what would you do? How would you want to bring it about that in the world, in every country, in every province, in every community no one hungers any more, no one freezes, no man, no woman and no child is undernourished? To speak only of the most elementary needs! And what if the revolution broke out in a single country? What good could it do? What goal could it aim for?*

Things are no longer such that one can say to the men of a nation: Your soil produces what you need in food and raw materials of industry: work and exchange! Unite, you poor men, give credit to each other; credit, mutuality is capital; you need no money-capitalists and no entrepreneurial masters; work in city and country: work and exchange!

Things are no longer such, even if the moment could be expected when great, comprehensive measures would affect the whole.

A tremendous confusion, a truly bestial chaos, a childish helplessness would arise at the moment of a revolution. Never were men more dependent and weaker than now when capitalism has reached its height! the world market of profit and the proletariat.

No world statistic and no world republic can help us. *Salvation can come only from the rebirth of the peoples out of the spirit of community!*

The basic form of socialist culture is the league of communities with independent economies and exchange system.

Our human prosperity, our existence now depends on the fact that the unity of the individual and the unity of the family, which are the only natural groups that have survived, is again intensified to the unity of communities, the basic form of every society.

If we want a society, then we must construct it, we must practice it.

Society is a society of societies of societies; a league of leagues of leagues; a commonwealth of commonwealths of commonwealths; a republic of republics of republics. Only there is freedom and order, only there is spirit, a spirit which is self-sufficiency and community,

unity and independence.

The independent individual, who lets no one interfere in his business; for whom the house community of the family, with home and work-place, is his world; the autonomous local community; the county or group of communities, and so on, ever more broadly with the more comprehensive groups that have an ever smaller number of duties — that is what a society looks like, that alone is socialism, which is worth working for, which can save us from our misery. Futile and wrong are the attempts to further expand in states and groups of states the coercive system of government that is today a surrogate for the absent free-spirited unity, and to extend their sphere still further into the field of economics than had previously happened. This police socialism that suffocates every original quality and activity, would seal the complete ruin of our peoples, and would hold together the fully scattered atoms by a mechanically iron ring. A natural unity can be attained by us men only where we are in local proximity, in real contact. In the family, the uniting spirit, the union of several persons for a common task, and for a common purpose, has too narrow and scanty a form for communal life. The family is concerned only with private interests. We need a natural core of the common spirit for public life so that public life will no longer be filled and led exclusively by the state and coldness as till now, but by a warmth akin to family affection. This core of all genuine communal life is the local community, the economic community, whose essence no one can imagine who seeks to judge if, for instance, by what today calls itself "community."

The capital used for the factories, for the processing of raw materials, the transportation of freight and passengers, is in reality nothing else but common spirit. Hunger, hands and earth — all three are there, they exist by nature: the hands industriously procure for hunger the needed goods out of the earth. In addition there is the special experience of certain regions in centuries-old trades; the particular constitution of the soil, so that certain raw materials can be found only in particular places, the necessity and convenience of trade. Let men exchange from community to community what neither can nor should be produced locally, as within the communities they trade from individual to individual. Let them trade one product for an equivalent product and in every community each one will have as much to consume as he wants, i.e., as he works.

Hunger, hands and earth are there, all three are there by nature. And besides them men need only regulate decently what goes on between them and they will have what they need so that each one can work only for himself; so that they all exploit nature but not one another. That is the task of socialism: to arrange the exchange economy so that each one even under a trading system works only for himself; so that men stand in thousandfold association with one another and yet nothing in this union is taken away from anyone, but to each is given. It will be given not as a gift from one person to another; socialism intends neither renunciation nor robbery; each receives the output of his work and enjoys the strengthening of all by the division of labor, exchange and a working communality in extracting the products of nature.

Hunger, hands and earth are there; all three exist by nature. Strange that men in city and country today must be told as something new that everything that enters into our consumption, except air, stems from the earth and from plants and animals that grow on the earth.

Hunger, hands and earth are there; all three are there by nature. We feel hunger daily and reach into our pockets to get money, the means to buy and the means to satisfy it. What is here called hunger, is every real need; to satisfy each we reach into our coffers for money.

To obtain money we sell or rent ourselves. We move our hands, and what is here called hands, is the many muscles, nerves and brain, is spirit and body, is work. Work on the soil; work under the earth; work for the further processing of products of the earth; work in exchange and transportation; work to enrich the rich; work for pleasure and instruction; work to educate youth; work that produces harmful, useless and worthless things; work that produces nothing and is done only for the gawkers to see. Many things today are called work; today everything that brings in money is called work.

Hunger, hands and earth are there; all three are there by nature. Where is the earth? The earth that our hands need to still our hunger.

A few men own the earth, and they have become fewer and fewer.

Capital, as we said, is not a thing but a spirit between us. We have the means for industry and trade, if only we have rediscovered ourselves and our human nature. The earth, however, is a piece of external nature. It is part of nature like air and light; the earth belongs inalienably to all men; and the earth has become private property, owned by only a few!

All ownership of things, all land-ownership is in reality ownership of men. Whoever withholds the earth from others, from the masses, forces these others to work for him. Private ownership is theft and slave-holding.

Through the money-economy, such has become land-ownership that does not appear so. In the just exchange economy, I have, in effect, a share in the soil, even if I own no land; in the money-economy in the land of profit, usury, interest, you are in reality a land-thief even if you own no land, but only money and stocks. In the just economy, where a product is exchanged for an equivalent product, I work daily for myself even if nothing I make enters into my own use; in the money economy in the land of profit, you are a slave-master even if you do not employ a single worker, as long as you live from anything else than the results of your work. And even if someone lives only from the results of his work, he participates in the exploitation of men if his work is a monopolized and privileged one and attains a higher price than it is worth.

Hunger, hands and earth are there; all three are there by nature.

We must have the earth again. The communities of socialism must redistribute the land. The earth is no one's private property. Let the earth have no masters; then we men are free.

The communities of socialism must redistribute the earth. Does property once again come about thereby?

I know very well that others picture common ownership or non-domination differently. They see everything in a fog: I try to see clearly. They see everything in the perfection of a described ideal; I want to express what can be done now and anytime. Now and anytime things will not go hazily and indefinitely in this world; socialism is the task at hand. Whoever wants to realize it must know what he wants now. Now and anytime the radical transformer will find nothing to transform except what is there. Therefore it will be good now and anytime for the local community to own its common property; that a part be the common land and other parts the family property for house, yard, garden and field.

Even the abolition of private property will essentially be a transformation of our spirit. Out of this rebirth a mighty redistribution of property will follow, and in connection with this redistribution there will be the permanent intention to redistribute the land in future times at definite or indefinite intervals again and again.

Justice will always depend on the spirit that prevails between men, and anyone who thinks that a spirit is now necessary and possible that would so crystallize into form as to attain something permanent and leave nothing for the future does not know the spirit of socialism at all. The spirit is always moving and creating; and what it creates will always be inadequate, and never will perfection become an event except as an image or idea. It would be a futile and misguided effort to want to create standard institutions once and for all, that would automatically exclude every possibility for exploitation and usury. Our times have shown what results when automatically functioning institutions replace the living spirit. Let every generation provide bravely and radically for what corresponds to their spirit. There must still be reason enough for revolutions later; and they become necessary when new spirit must turn against rigid residues of fled spirit. Thus the struggle against private property will probably lead to completely different results than many, e.g., the so-called Communists, probably believe. Private property is not the same thing as ownership; and I see in the future private ownership, cooperative ownership, community ownership in most beautiful flowering; ownership by no means only of the objects of direct use or the simplest tools, but also the so superstitiously feared ownership of means of production of all sorts, houses and land. No final security measures for the millennium or for eternity are to be made, but a great, comprehensive equalization and the creation of the will to repeat this equalization periodically.

"Then you are to sound the trumpet throughout your land on the tenth day of the seventh month as the day of equalization...

"And you are to sanctify the fiftieth year and proclaim a free year in the land to all that dwell therein; for it is your year of jubilee; then everyone among you is to come back to his property and to his family.

"That is the jubilee year, when every man is to regain what belongs to him."

Let him who has ears, hear.

You shall sound the trumpet through all your land!

The voice of the spirit is the trumpet that will sound again and again and again, as long as men are together. Injustice will always seek to perpetuate itself; and always as long as men are truly alive, revolt against it will break out.

Revolt as constitution; transformation and revolution as a rule established once and for all; order through the spirit as intention; that was the great and sacred heart of the Mosaic social order.

We need that again: a new rule and transformation by the spirit, which will not establish things and institutions in a final form, but will declare itself as permanently at work in them. Revolution must be a part of our social order, must become the basic rule of our constitution. The spirit will create forms for itself, forms of movement, not of rigidity; ownership that does not become private property, that provides only the possibility to work with security but not the possibility of exploitation and arrogance; a means of exchange that has no value of itself but only in relation to trade, but also contains the conditions for its use; a means of exchange that can expire and precisely therefore can vivify, whereas today it is immortal and murderous.

Instead of having life among us, we have set death between us. Everything was reduced to a thing and an objective idol. Confidence and mutuality degenerated into capital. Common interest was replaced by the state. Our attitude, our relationships became rigid conditions, and with terrible contortions and upheavals here and there after long lapses of time a revolution broke out, which in turn produced death and institutions and firm, unchangeable realities, which it died of before it lived. Let us now do a complete job by establishing in our economy the only principle that can be established, the principle that corresponds to the basic socialist insight: that no greater consumer value shall enter a house than was produced by work in that house, because no value originates in the world of men except through work alone. Whoever wishes to give up or make a present of anything may do so, that is his good right and does not concern the economy, but no one should be forced to do without things because of circumstances. Yet the means for implementing this principle ever anew will always be different everywhere, and the principle will live only as long as it is reapplied again and again.

The Marxists have regarded the earth as a sort of appendage to capital and never quite knew what to do with it. In reality capital is composed of two quite different things: first, land and the products of the soil, lots, buildings, machines, tools, which however should not be called "capital" because they are part of the land; secondly, relationship between men, a uniting spirit. Money, or the means of exchange, is nothing more than a conventional sign for the general commodity with the help of which all particular commodities can be conveniently traded, i.e., in this case, directly for the other.

This does not directly have anything to do with capital. Capital is not a means of exchange and not a sign but a possibility. The particular capital of a working man or a group of working men is their possibility to produce certain products in a certain time. The material realities that are used for this are, first, the materials—the land and the products of the land—from which new products are to be further processed; secondly, the tools, which are worked with, i.e., also products of the land; thirdly, the needs of life which are consumed by the workers during the time of work, again products of the land. As long as one is working only at one product he cannot exchange that product for what he needs during production and for it; but all working men are in this situation of expectation and tension. Capital, now, is merely the anticipation and advance payment of the expected product, is precisely the same as credit or mutuality. In the just exchange economy every person who has work-requests or every production group that has customers receives the material means, the earth and the products of the earth for its hunger and its hands: because all have the corresponding needs and each provides the other with the realities that have themselves resulted from expectation and tension, so that once again possibility and readiness will be changed to reality, and so on. Capital is thus not a thing; the land and its products are the thing. The conventional view is a completely impermissible and bitterly wrong duplication of the world of things, as if besides the one and only world of the land there were also the world of capital as a thing. Thus, possibility, which is only a relationship of tension, is changed into a reality. There is only one objective reality, the land. Everything else that is usually called capital is relation, movement, circulation, possibility, tension, credit or, as we call it, the unifying spirit in its economic function, which will of course not make its appearance amateurishly as love and obligingness, but will use purposeful organs, one of which Proudhon described as an exchange bank.

When we call the present time the capitalist age, this expression means that the unifying spirit no longer prevails in the economy, but that the object-idol rules, i.e., something that is not really a thing, but a nothing, that is mistaken for a thing.

This nothing that is considered to be a thing does bring many concrete realities into the rich man's house, because what is considered so [*Geltung*] is money [*Geld*], and into a position of power, all of which does not stem from nothing but from the land and the work of the poor. For whenever work seeks to approach the land and whenever a product wants to go from one stage of labor to another and before it may enter the consumer sector, false capital inserts itself into the whole process of work and does not take merely the payment for its small services, but on top of this the interest because it was so willing not to lie still but to circulate.

Another nothing that is considered a thing and replaces the missing spirit of unity, is, as was already often mentioned above, the state. It steps in everywhere as a hindrance, pushing, sucking and pressing between men and men, between men and the land, wherever the genuine link between men has been weakened: mutual attraction and relationship, a free spirit. This also has to do with the fact that the ungenuine capital, which has replaced genuine mutual interest and trust could not exercise its vampire-like plundering power, that land-ownership could not impose its tribute, if it were not supported by force, by the power of the state, its laws, its administration and executive. But one should never forget that all this—state, laws, administration and executives—are only names for men, who because they lack the possibilities of life, torment and do violence to one another, i.e., names for force between men.

So we see in this passage, after the right explanation of capital has been given that the term "capital" is not quite accurate, because it designates not genuine capital, but the false one. But it cannot be voided, when one wishes to disentangle the true connections for men, to first use the accepted words, and that is what happened here.

Thus when the workers find that they have no capital, they are right in quite a different sense than they think. They are lacking the capital of capitals, the only capital that is a reality — reality although it is not a thing — they are lacking the spirit. And like all who have become dishabituated from this possibility and precondition of all life, in addition the material condition of all life has been whisked away from under their feet: namely the land.

Land and spirit therefore — that is socialism's solution.

Men seized by the spirit will first look around for land as the only external condition which they need for society.

We know very well that when men exchange their products in their world economy and their national economy, land too is thereby made mobile. Land has long since been converted into a stock-market object, into paper. We also know that if men would, in their world market and their national market, exchange one product for an equivalent one, i.e., if large groups would enable themselves, by uniting their consumption and the extraordinary credit that would, no doubt, result, they would be able to produce an ever increasing quantity of industrial products for their own use from new materials without resorting to the capitalist market. We know that they then would, in the course of time, be able to buy not only products of the land, but, increasingly, the land itself. We know that such mighty consumer-producer-associations would dispose not only over their own mutual credit, but finally also over considerable monetary capital. But if men were satisfied with only that, they would have merely postponed the final decision. The land-owners have a monopoly of everything that grows on the land or is obtained from under the land: on the food of the entire people and the industrial raw materials. The foundations of the state and of an ever larger part of money-capital are undermined when private ownership of the land is abolished and mutuality introduced as the socialist form of capital, but before this point is reached, the more capitalist trade and industry are eliminated by the consumer-producer-cooperatives, the more strongly the state and money-capitalism will side with the land-magnates. The landed sector will not automatically supply the cooperatives working for their own consumption, rather it will raise the price of its products to almost prohibitive levels. For land is only apparently fluid or paper, just as *vice versa* capital is a real magnitude only fictionally At the moment of decision, land becomes what it really is: a piece of physical nature that is owned and withheld.

Socialists cannot avoid the struggle against landownership. *The struggle for socialism is a struggle for the land; the social question is an agrarian question.*

Now it can be seen what an enormous mistake the Marxists' theory of the proletariat is. *If the revolution came today, no stratum of the population would have less idea of what to do than our industrial proletarians.* Very attractive, of course, to their longing for release—for they do long for release and rest, but they have little idea of what new relationships and conditions they want to establish—is Herwegh's old slogan: "Man of work, wake up! Know your strength! All wheels stand still, if your strong arm will." This saying is enticing, as is everything that gives a general expression to facts, and so is logical. That the general strike would have to produce a terrible chaos, that the capitalists would have to surrender if the workers could endure even for a very short time, is quite true.

But that is a big "if," and the workers today hardly have a clear enough picture of the tremendous difficulties of providing themselves with food in case of a revolutionary general strike. Still, a sudden, comprehensive, general strike with violent thrust could unquestionably give decisive power to the revolutionary unions. On the day after the revolution, the unions would occupy the factories and workshops in the big industrial cities, and would have to continue producing the identical products for the world profit-market, they would divide the savings and profits among themselves—and be surprised that the only result was a worsening of their situation, a stoppage of production and complete impossibility.

It has become completely impossible to transfer the exchange economy of profit-capitalism directly into the socialist exchange economy. That it cannot be done all at once is self-evident; if an attempt were made to implement it gradually, the results would be a most terrible fragmentation of the revolution, the wildest struggles between the rapidly ensuing parties, economic chaos, and political despotism.

We are much too far removed from justice and reason in the manufacturing and distribution of products. Every consumer is today dependent on the entire world economy, because the profit economy has been interposed between him and his needs. The eggs I eat come from Galicia, the butter from Denmark, the meat from Argentina, and the grain for my bread also from America, the wool for my suit from Australia, the cotton of my shirt, the leather and the necessary tanning materials for my boots, the wood for table, chairs and desks, etc. all from America.

The men of our time have lost their relationships and become irresponsible. Relationship is an attraction that brings people together and enables them to work together to supply their needs. This relationship, without which we are not living men, has been externalized and reified. The merchant doesn't care who buys his products; the proletarian doesn't care what he makes or works at; the enterprise does not have the natural purpose of satisfying needs, but the artificial one of acquiring things, in as big quantities as possible, without consideration of, and as much as possible without work, i.e., through the work of other subjected people, through money, which can satisfy all needs. Money has swallowed up relationships and is therefore much more than a thing. The mark of a purposeful thing, that was processed artificially out of nature, is that it no longer grows, that it cannot draw materials or energies out of the surrounding world, but that it calmly waits for consumption and spoils sooner or later, if it is not used. What grows has self-movement, and self-generation, is an organism. And so money is an artificial organism; it grows, it produces offspring, it multiplies wherever it is, and is immortal.

Fritz Mauthner (*Dictionary of Philosophy*) has shown that the word "God" was originally identical with "idol" and that both mean "poured (metal)." God is a product made by men that comes to life, draws the life of men to itself and finally becomes more powerful than all mankind.

The only "poured metal," the only idol, the only God that men have ever created physically is money. Money is artificial and alive, money breeds money, and money and money and money has all power on earth.

Who however fails to see, still fails to see today that money, this God, is nothing else but spirit that has exited from man and become a living thing, an un-thing, that it is the meaning of life changed to madness? Money does not create wealth, money is wealth; wealth *per se*; there is no one rich except money. Money gets its powers and its life from somewhere; it can get them only from us; and as rich and generatively productive as we have made money, we have impoverished and sapped ourselves, all of us. It has almost become literally true that human women by the hundreds of thousands can no longer become mothers because hideous money bears offspring and hard metal like a vampire sucks the animal warmth out of men and women and the blood out of their veins. We are all beggars and poor wretches and fools, because money is God, and because money has become cannibalistic.

Socialism is a reversal of this. Socialism is a new beginning. Socialism is a return to nature, a re-endowment with spirit, a regaining of relationships.

There is no other way to socialism than for us to learn and practice why we are working. We are not working for the God or devil to whom the men of today have sold their souls, but for our needs. The restoration of the link between work and consumption: that is socialism. The God has now become so powerful and almighty that it no longer can be abolished by a mere technical change, by a reform of the exchange system.

Socialists therefore must form new communities that produce what their members need.

We cannot wait for mankind, nor can we wait until mankind is united, for a common economy and a just exchange system, as long as we have not found and re-created humanity in us as individuals.

Everything begins with the individual, and everything depends on the individual. Compared with what surrounds and shackles us today, socialism is the most gigantic task men have ever undertaken. It cannot be realized by external cures involving coercion or cleverness.

As a starting point we can use many things that still contain some life, external forms of living spirit. Village communities with remnants of the old common property, with the farmers' and field workers' memories of the original common property which passed into private ownership centuries ago as well as customs recalling the common economy for work in the fields and in the crafts. Farmer's blood still flows in the veins of many urban proletarians; they should learn to listen to it again. The goal, the still very remote goal is what is today called the general strike, i.e., the refusal to work for others, for the rich, for the idols and the monstrosity. The general strike—but of course a different one than the passive general strike with arms crossed, which is proclaimed today and with a defiance whose momentary success is very uncertain and whose ultimate failure is absolutely certain, calls to the capitalists: "Let us see who can hold out the longest!" A general strike, yes! but an active one, with a very different activity than is sometimes associated with the revolutionary general strike, which in plain language is called "plundering." The active general strike will be victorious only when the working men are able to refuse to give one bit of their activity, their work, to others, but work only for their own needs, their real needs. That is still a long way off—but who is not aware that we are still far from socialism, but just beginning a long, long road? That is why we are mortal enemies of Marxism: because it has kept the working men from beginning with socialism. The magic word that leads us out of the petrified world of greed and hardship is not "strike"—but "work."

Agriculture, industry and crafts, mental and physical work, teaching and apprenticeship system must be re-united; Peter Kropotkin has said very valuable things about the methods for achieving this in his book, *Field, Factory and Workshop*.

We must not give up our hope in the people, the whole people, all our peoples. Of course, there are today no peoples. The state and money have replaced the people, i.e., men united by spirit, while individuals have been reduced to disjunct human fragments.

The people can be restored to existence, only when individuals, progressive and spiritual, again are filled with the spirit of the people, when a preliminary form of the people lives in creative men and demands realization in reality by their hearts, heads, and hands.

Socialism is not a science, although it does require all sorts of knowledge—a necessary condition of giving up superstition and false living in favor of treading the right path. However, socialism is certainly an art, a new art that seeks to build with living material.

Men and women of all classes are now called upon to leave the people in order to come to the people.

For that is the task: not to despair of the people, but also not to wait for the people. Whoever does justice to the quintessence of the people he bears inside him, whoever joins together with others like himself for the sake of this unborn seed and pressing, imaginary form to transform into reality whatever can be done to realize the socialist order, leaves the people to go to the people.

Socialism will become a different reality depending on the number that join together for it, people who feel the deepest repugnance for existing injustice and have the strongest desire and yearning for a true formation of society.

So let us unite to establish socialist households, socialist villages, socialist communities.

Culture is not based on any particular forms of technology or satisfaction of needs, but on the spirit of justice.

Whoever wants to do something for socialism, must set to work out of a premonition of an intuited, yet unknown joy and happiness. We still have everything to learn: the joy of work, of common interest, of mutual forbearance. We have forgotten everything, yet we still sense it all in us.

These settlements in which socialists cut themselves off as much as possible from the capitalist market and export only as much value as still has to come in from the outside are only small beginnings and trials. They should shine out over the country, so that the masses of men will be overcome by envy of the new primeval bliss of satisfaction with oneself, of joyfulness in the heart of the community.

Socialism as reality can only be learned; socialism is, like all life, an attempt. Everything that we try to frame poetically in words and descriptions: variety in work, the role of mental work, the form of the most convenient and least questionable means of exchange, the introduction of the contract instead of law, the renewal of education, all that will become reality in the act of being realized and by no means will be arranged according to a predetermined pattern.

Conceivably we will then remember those who in thought and

imagination anticipated and foresaw communities and lands of socialism in articulated forms. Reality will look different than their individual formations, but reality will stem from these images of theirs.

Let us here recall Proudhon and all his sharply defined, never nebulous visions from the land of freedom and the contract. Let us remember many good things seen and described by Henry George, Michael Flürscheim, Silvio Gesell, Ernst Busch, Peter Kropotkin, Elisée Reclus, and many others.

We are the heirs of the past, whether we like it or not; let us muster the will to have coming generations be our heirs, so that in all our life and actions we influence the coming generations and the masses of men around us.

This is a completely new socialism, one that is new again; new for our time, new in expression, new in its view of the past, new also in many of its moods. We also have to take a new look at what exists: we must look again at the classes of men, the institutions and traditions. We now see the peasants in a completely new light and we know what an enormous task has been left to us, to speak to them, live among them, and revive and resuscitate in them what has wilted and atrophied: religion, not faith in any external or higher power, but faith in their own strength and in the perfectibility of the individual human being as long as he lives. How the peasant and his love for ownership of the soil has been feared: the peasants do not have too much land, but too little, and it must not be taken away but given to them. But, of course, what they, like everyone else, need most of all is a common, communal spirit. However this spirit is not buried over so much in them as it is in the urban workers. Socialist settlers need only go and live in the existing villages and it will be seen that they can be revived and the spirit that was in them in the fifteenth and sixteenth centureis can re-awaken even today.

One must speak of this socialism to men, with new tongues. Here a first, initial attempt is made. We will learn to do it better, we and others. We want to bring to socialism the cooperatives, which are socialist form without spirit, and to the trade unions, which are courage without a goal.

Whether we want to or not, we will not stop with talk; we will go further. We no longer believe in a gap between the present and the future; we know: America is here or nowhere!" What we do not do now, at this moment, we do not do at all.

We can unite our consumption and eliminate all sorts of parasites. We can establish a great number of crafts and industries to produce goods for our own consumption. We can go much further in this than the cooperatives have gone until now, for they still cannot get rid of the idea of competing with capitalist-managed enterprise. They are bureaucratic, they are centralistic; and they cannot help themselves except by becoming employers and closing contracts with their employees through the medium of the trade unions. It does not occur to them that in the consumer-producer-cooperative each one works for himself in a genuine exchange economy; that in it not the profitability but the productivity of work is decisive; that many forms of enterprise, e.g., the small enterprise, are thoroughly productive and welcome in socialism, though unprofitable under capitalism.

We can establish settlements, though they will not escape completely from capitalism at one stroke. But we now know that socialism is a road, a road away from capitalism, and that every road has a beginning. Socialism will not grow out of capitalism, but away from it; it will barricade itself off from it.

The means to purchase land and the first operating funds for these settlements will be obtained by pooling together our consumption, through trade unions and worker groups that join with us, and through such rich men as either join us completely or at least contribute to our cause. I do not hesitate to expect all this and to proclaim this expectation. Socialism is the cause of all who suffer under the terrible conditions in and around us; and many of all classes will soon endure far greater suffering than anyone suspects today. No one, including the workers' associations, can do anything better in the sense of decency and his own redemption, with his money, than to give it away once and for all and liberate the land with it for the beginning of socialism. Once the land is free, no one will be able to tell—it itself won't even feel it—that it has been bought. Don't be squeamish, you workers: you buy shoes, pants, potatoes, herrings; wouldn't it be a beautiful beginning if you, working and suffering men, no matter what roles have been your lot til now, would pool together your strength, to purchase your own liberation from injustice and from now on to make what you need, for your own community, on your own land?

Let us not forget: if we are in the right spirit, then we have everything we need for society except one thing: land. Hunger for land must come over you, you men of the big city!

Once socialist colonies with their own culture are scattered everywhere in the land, north, south, east and west, in all provinces amid the baseness of the profit-economy, and they are seen, their joy in life, in its inexpressible though quiet manner, is felt, then envy will become greater and greater. Then, I believe, the people will move. The people will begin to see, to know, to be certain. Only one thing is missing in externals, to live socialistically, prosperously, blissfully: the land. And then the peoples will set the land free and no longer work for the false god but for men. Then! Just begin; start on the smallest scale and with the smallest number of men.

The state, i.e., the still ignorant masses, the privileged classes, and the representatives of both, the executive and administrative caste, will place the greatest and smallest obstacles in the way of the beginners. We know that.

All these impediments, if they are real ones, will be destroyed if we stand so close together that not the tiniest space is left between them and ourselves. Now they are only obstacles in anticipation, imagination, fear. We see it now: when the time comes they will barricade our path with all sorts of obstacles—and so in the meantime we choose to do nothing.

We'll cross that bridge when we come to it! Let us move ahead, so that we will become many.

No one can do violence to the people, except this people itself.

And great parts of our people side with injustice and what harms them in body and soul, because our spirit is not strong and convincing enough.

Our spirit must ignite, illuminate, entice and attract.

Talk alone never does this; even the mightiest, angriest or gentlest talk does not.

Only example can do it.

We must give the example and lead the way.

Example and spirit of sacrifice! In the past, today and tomorrow, sacrifice upon sacrifice will be made to the idea, always in revolt due to the impossibility of continuing to live this way.

Now it is necessary to make other kinds of sacrifices, not heroic ones, but quiet, unimpressive sacrifices in order to give an example for the right way of life.

Then the few will become many, and the many will also become few. Hundreds, thousands, hundreds of thousands—too few, too few!

Still the obstacles will be overcome; for whoever builds in the right spirit, destroys the strongest obstacles by building.

And finally, finally socialism, which has glowed and flamed for so long, finally it will cast light. And men and peoples will know with great certainty: they have socialism and the means to realize it, completely and totally in themselves, among them, and they lack only one thing: land! And they will set the land free; for no one impedes the people anymore, since the people no longer stands in its own way.

I call on all those who want to do what they can to build this socialism. Only the present is real, and what men do not do now, do not begin to do immediately they will not do in all eternity. The objective is people, society, community, freedom, beauty, and joy of life. We need men to give the battle-cry; we need all who are filled with this creative desire; we need men of action. This call to socialism is addressed to men of action who want to make the first beginning.

Whoever has not already heard it in the hours when these words and the feeling behind them were addressed to him, let it now be said to him in parting: just as we have voiced many a familiar idea in order for men to be able to understand us, and then rejected such provisory, current words as falsely applied or inadequate, the same may happen to this word: socialism. Perhaps this call is also the beginning of a way to find a better, deeper, and more promising word. Each one ought to know already: our socialism has nothing in common with sumptuous ease or the desire for a pastoral, idyllic peace and a broad life devoted only to the economy and to working only for the needs of life. There was much talk here of the economy; it is the basis of our very life and should become so much so that less talk about it will be needed. Greetings, you restless wanderers, hobos and vagabonds, who can bear no economy and no place in this our time. Greetings, you artists, whose creativity transcends the time. Greetings, you warriors of old, who did not want life to shrivel up in the stove-pipe! What there is in the world today of war, sabre-rattling and wildness is almost entirely only the grotesque mask of desolation and greed; stature, fidelity and knightliness have become preciously scanty. Greetings, you stammerers, you silent ones, who have an intimation deep in your hearts, where no word rolls out: unknown greatness, unspoken struggles, deep suffering of soul, wild joys and sorrows will from now on be mankind's lot, both for individuals and peoples.

You painters, poets, muscians, you know of it and the voices of power and ardour and sweetness that will bloom forth from new peoples already speak from you. Scattered in all our desolation, young men live, solid men, old men, tried and tested, noble women; more than they themselves know, men live here and there who have childlike hearts. In all of them there lives faith and the certainty of great joy and great sufering that will one day seize men anew and shape them and drive them forwards. Pain, holy pain: come o come into our hearts! where you are not, there can never be peace. All you—or are you then so few?—all in whom the dream smiles and weeps, all who breathe action, who feel jubilation deep within you, all who wish to despair for cause and madness and real distress, not for the slovenly nonsense and baseness around us today, that are called misery and hardship, all who are lonesome today and contain an inner form, image and rhythm of pent-up creative energy in you, all who can give the command from your hearts: in the name of eternity, in the name of spirit, in the name of the image that seeks to become a true path, mankind shall not perish. The gray-green, thick mud that is today sometimes called proletariat, sometimes bourgeois, sometimes the ruling caste, and everywhere, above and below is nothing but a disgusting mass, this horribly repulsive human distortion of greed, satiety, degradation, shall no longer twist and turn, shall no longer be allowed to dirty and suffocate us: they all are called to socialism.

This is a first word. Much still has to be said. It shall be said. By me and by others who are called here.

THE 12 ARTICLES OF THE SOCIALIST FEDERATION

(June 14, 1908)

Article 1
The basic form of socialist culture is the federation of independently managed economic communities trading together in justice.

Article 2
This Socialist Federation, following the path shown by history, replaces governments and the capitalist economy.

Article 3
The Socialist Federation accepts as the goal of its efforts the word republic in its original meaning: the cause of the common good.

Article 4
The Socialist Federation declares the goal of its efforts to be anarchy in its original meaning: order through voluntary associations.

Article 5
The Socialist Federation includes all working men who want the social order of the Socialist Federation. Its task is neither proletarian politics nor class war, which are both necessary accessories of capitalism and the power-state, but struggle and organization for socialism.

Article 6
The real effectiveness of the Socialist Federation can begin only when greater portions of the masses have joined it. Until then its task is propaganda and composure.

Article 7
The members of the Socialist Federation want to put their work in the service of their consumption.

Article 8
They combine their power of consumption to exchange the products of their work with the help of their exchange bank.

Article 9
They send ahead pioneers to inland settlements of the Socialist Federation to produce everything themselves as far as possible, including the products of the earth.

Article 10
Culture is not based on any particular forms of technology or of satisfying needs, but on the spirit of justice.

Article 11
These settlements are to be only models of justice and joyous work: not means to attain the goal. The goal can be attained only when the land comes into the hands of the socialists by means other than purchase.

Article 12
The Socialist Federation aims for the right and hence the power to abolish private ownership of the land at the time of transition by great fundamental measures, and to give all citizens the possibility to live in culture and happiness by combining industry and agriculture in independently operated trading communities on the basis of justice.

NAME INDEX

Friedrich Adler 1897-1960: 19

Son of Victor Adler, the main leader of the Austrian Socialists before World War I. During the war, Friedrich Adler was one of the leading minds of the socialist left within the Austrian workers' movement. In 1916, as an opponent of his military policy, he shot to death the Austrian Minister President Count Stürgkh for which he was sentenced to death but was not executed. After 1918 Adler was first a representative of the Workers' Councils, later secretary of the "International Socialist Worker Parties" (ISAP).

Kurt Eisner 1867-1916: 19

For a time before World War I, he was editor of *Vorwärts*. As a historian, he is remembered for his important biography of Wilhelm Liebknecht. Under arrest from January 1918 to October 1918 for his part in a munitions workers' strike, he played a decisive role in the outbreak of the Bavarian Revolution. Eisner was shot to death in 1919 by Count Arco-Valley on the way to the opening of the *Landtag*.

Petr Alexejevich Kropotkin, Prince 1842-1921: 25, 137

Originally a Czarist officer and important scientific traveler, Kropotkin later became a leading representative of anarchism with his idea of "mutual help." Common ownership of the means of production and consumption are a part of his social ideas, and , at the same time, he advocated a federative principle directed against the idea of government. Shortly before his death, he returned to Russia after a long exile. Among his main works are *Ethics, Mutual Aid, Memories of a Revolutionary* (2 vols.)

Karl Kautsky 1854-1938: 44

The major theorist of orthodox Marxism, author of the "Erfurt Program," founder and editor-in-chief (1883-1917) of the leading socialist theoretical journal: *Die Neue Zeit*. Firm opponent of Russian Bolshevism, but also of Eduard Bernstein and Rosa Luxemburg. Main work: *The Materialist Conception of History* (2 vols.).

Pierre Joseph Proudhon 1809-1865: 61, 62, 84, 104, 107, 108, 109, 117, 119, 122, 139

French Socialist who lived most of his life in exile in Belgium. Developed, at times in violent controversy with Marx, a social order based on a system of mutual services (mutualism). He rejected governmental coercion and was an opponent of every kind of centralism. Proposed the establishment of an exchange bank to implement his ideas. Main works: *On the Federative Principle, System of Economic Contradictions: or Philosophy of Misery*.

Michail Alexandrovich Bakunin 1814-1876: 63

Russian anarchist. Politically active in France, Switzerland and Germany until his extradition to Czarist Russia in 1851, and was exiled to Siberia in 1857. In 1860, he made a dramatic escape by way of the Far East to London. He participated in the first "Socialist International," but was expelled in 1872. Works: *State and Anarchy, God and the State*.

Giuseppe Garibaldi 1807-1882: 62, 63

A leader of militant Italian leftist liberalism, he became extremely important for Italy's development into a unified country as the military commander of a corps of volunteers.

Adam Smith 1723-1790: 65

The founder of modern liberal economic theory. He felt that the driving force is man's drive to improve his own situation; hence, the good of the whole is attained by way of the individual's egoism. Free competition leads to social harmony and state interference should be kept to a minimum. Smith calls for free trade and an international division of labor. Main works: *Theory of moral sentiments, An inquiry into the nature and causes of the wealth of nations.*

David Ricardo 1772-1823: 65
For a time a member of Parliament, Ricardo developed, under Smith's influence, a complete system of economics. Stressing the principle of economic freedom, especially of free trade, he recognized work as the main factor of production. His concept of work later became important for Marx. Main work: *On the principles of political economy and taxation.*

Clara Zetkin (née Eissner) 1857-1933: 76
A leading German socialist woman politician and later a leading German Communist. For many years she served as editor of the socialist women's journal *Die Gleichheit* (Equality). In 1932 she was a senior member of the German Reichstag and later died in exile in the Soviet Union. Main work: *Reden und Schriften (Speeches and Writings)* published by the Institute for Marxism-Leninism in 1957.

Emile de Girardin 1806-1881: 89
French journalist and newspaper publisher who was one of the founders of the modern big-city press.

Moritz von Egidy 1847-1898: 91
The advocate of an undogmatic, purely humanitarian Christianity who retired from the Prussian army as a lieutenant colonel. From 1894 he published the socialist-anarchist journal *Versöhnung (Reconciliation)*. Writings: *United Christianity.*

Heinrich von Reder 1824-1909: 92
Story-writer and lyric poet with a strong regard for nature that held a clear trace of pessimism. Main work: *Lyrical Sketchbook.*

Christian Wagner 1835-1918: 92
A farmer and lyric poet with a strong sense of nature which combined with a mystical world view and interpretation of life. *Selected Poems* were published by Hermann Hesse.

Eugen Dühring 1833-1921: 110

University lecturer and private scholar in Berlin, 1864-1877. He worked in the areas of ethics, economic theory and general social sciences and also was noted as a philosopher. His views are very varied with positivistic elements being quite discernible, but his concept of "anticratism" comes very close to anarchist trains of thought. Main work: *The Value of Life*. Dühring also became known through his controversy with Engels. See also, Fr. Engels, *Mr. Eugen Dühring's Revolution of Science*.

Silvio Gesell 1862-1930: 119, 139

A monetary reformer and Bavarian finance minister during the Workers' Council Republic. He saw economic crises to be avoidable through the use of temporary money. The creation of a currency with stable buying power and the problem of land reform constitute the core of his thought. Main work: *Natural Economic Order through Free Land and Free Money*.

Fédéric Bastiat 1801-1850: 122

A liberal French economist of an optimistic and anti-socialist bent, he saw social harmony becoming possible by means of "laissez-faire." Main work: *Economic Harmonies*.

Fritz Mauthner 1849-1926: 135

A German linguist and historian of philosophy. Positivistic influences stemming from Mach are combined in Mauthner with a pronounced scepticism against all capacity for knowledge. He sees language and thought as almost identical, but man cannot grasp reality solely through his linguistic capacity. The ultimate realities are individualities, feelings and perception-contents. Mauthner is led by his theory into an objectless, atheistic mysticism in which elements of Spinoza are recognizable. Main works: *Contributions to a Critique of Language* (3 vols.), *Dictionary of Philosophy* (2 vols.), *Atheism and its History in the West* (4 vols.).

Henry George 1839-1897: 139

The American land-reformer with socialist tendencies, George sees private ground rents as the cause of misery; hence, the land should in principle belong to the state and only the harvest obtained from the land should belong to the producer. In Germany, Damaschke especially supported George. Main work: *Progress and Poverty.*

Michael Flürscheim 1844-1912: 139

A German land-reformer, very close to Henry George, he accepted private property in principle, but with considerable restrictions.

Ernst Busch 1851-1893: 139

Influenced by Proudhon, Ernst Busch developed mainly the idea of cooperatives, which he saw as the key to the solution of the social question. Main work: *The Solution of the Social Question.*

Elisée Reclus 1830-1905: 139

Reclus, one of the founders of modern geography and an internationally respected scientist, was at the same time one of the leading minds of French anarchism. He played an important part in the Paris Commune of 1871 and was a close friend of Kropotkin. Main work: *Evolution and Revolution.*